THE COMPLETE GUIDE TO CLEANSING AND DETOX

THE FOUR WINDS HOLISTIC CLEANSE

by

Nicholas Schnell,

RH (AHG), RD, LMNT

authorHOUSE®

AuthorHouse™
1663 Liberty Drive, Suite 200
Bloomington, IN 47403
www.authorhouse.com
Phone: 1-800-839-8640

First published by AuthorHouse 7/9/2008

ISBN: 978-1-4343-8986-2 (sc)

Printed in the United States of America
Bloomington, Indiana

This book is printed on acid-free paper.

ABOUT THE AUTHOR

Nicholas Schnell, RH (AHG), RD, LMNT has studied herbal medicine since the age of twelve. He is a clinical herbalist and clinical nutritionist in private practice in Omaha, Nebraska. He maintains a thriving alternative medicine clinic, helping those of all ages who suffer from a variety of diseases. His unique and diverse background integrates Native American, European, American, Traditional Chinese, Traditional Ayurvedic, and clinical approaches to herbal medicine. He is the founder of the Four Winds Center for Herbal Studies and faculty member at a variety of local colleges. Nicholas's passion for cleansing programs grew out of his observation of how drastically they improved his own health and the health of his patients. His decision to write this book was based on his concern for how much confusion there was regarding cleansing programs among the public and healthcare providers. His discovery of many unhealthy cleansing programs compelled him to share his vision and wisdom of detox therapies with the world.

Contacting the Author and Additional Information on Seasonal Cleansing

Visit the author's clinic website at *www.FourWindsNHC.com*. Extra books and cleansing products can be ordered from his on-line store at *www.cleansingdepot.com*. Nicholas can be contacted for professional lectures and workshops via email at spiritbear4@msn.com.

This book is dedicated to all who have lost their way in the suffering of illness.

May this book be a guide and inspiration to reclaim your birthrights of health, vitality and happiness.

"People pray to the gods for health, yet it is in their own hands to keep it. They do not consider that by their excesses they create the contrary and by their unchecked desires they betray their own health."

- Democritus

Contents

FOREWARD

Many of my best, early memories of studying natural medicine were the first liver cleanses I finished and how they made me feel renewed and refreshed like never before. But I also remember my sense of unease with many of the changes my body went through and how difficult it was to find reliable information. Every book or natural healer had a different answer. Numorous books I read were authored by people without experience or appropriate education. My college psychology professor told my class to read the forward of any book on child psychology. If the authors had not raised a child we were to throw it away because it was only theoretical and therefore useless. Here, that point of view is more than appropriate.

At the dawn of my practice ten years ago, I realized that Americans needed the knowledge of how to appropriately do a holistic cleanse program to regain their health. I saw how inspired people were to overcome their diseases just by taking a simple seasonal cleanse class. While working with these students, I realized even more how much harmful information there was. As I watched many follow different programs, I saw how they were not feeling better after they had finished. This was a clear sign something was wrong with their approach. It appeared as if most everyone was approaching cleansing without common sense or knowledge.

My patients and students sought help because they were attempting to overcome serious diseases like cancer or to repair the body after the destructive effects of chemotherapy. Many had serious or compromised toxic conditions like hepatitis, chronic pesticide exposure or heavy metal poisoning. Others simply wanted to be educated so they could embrace the wisdom of seasonal living and use cleansing as a key part of their preventative health programs. They began to request more detailed information on how cleansing worked and its many benefits.

My focus throughout has been on perfecting a cleansing program that would work for anyone. I found it was not an easy task. Some can't follow cleansing diets while others demand full strictness. Some had serious diseases that required only mild cleansing while others had illnesses that required greater intensity to speed the recovery process. In other cases, patients had either strong reactions or none at all.

The Four Winds Holistic Cleanse is the result of my observation, study of countless detox programs and passionate clinical experience supervising comprehensive whole body cleansing programs for hundreds of patients. It is the first truly holistic cleansing program in America that can be used in any season and at any stage of life. It is designed for almost everyone, creates dramatic health results and speeds up the body's rejuvenating process. It is easy to follow and inexpensive. Simply put, it is the only cleansing program you need to know to regain your health and vitality. Even though the cleanse focuses on getting results, there are many built in safety factors. This book details why one should cleanse, how to prepare, what to expect and how to get through the process without quitting. There are even chapters detailing how to keep your body healthy after your cleanse is completed and ways to create lasting lifestyle changes to minimize toxins in your family's daily life.

It also serves as a guide and brief encyclopedia to both healthcare providers and patients. Many patients may seek the advice of their healthcare provider before beginning a detox program. Unfortunately, many are also looking for reliable information – there are no classes in medical school on detoxification therapies. They may discourage one's desire to regain their health since they are similarly short on knowledge.

Whether you are a first time cleanser or have years of experience, this book is for you. Knowledge and understanding are half the battle to regaining health. Cleansing therapies are the quickest way to reverse disease and stimulate the body's healing abilities. Starting a cleanse is a process one needs to clearly understand before embarking on the journey. This book is a roadmap for everything you need to know along the way. In essence, this book is a guideline for healthy everyday living.

It has transformed my own personal health and the lives of many others. It is my vision it will do the same for you.

Nicholas Schnell
March, 2008

CHAPTER ONE

INTRODUCTION TO CLEANSING PROGRAMS

I was once doing a lecture when a doctor said that he didn't believe in cleansing or detox. My response was, "It is a good thing your liver still does, otherwise you would be dead within a few hours!" He was stunned because he knew I was right. I continued that every second of our life, the liver filters contaminants, metabolic byproducts, and food and toxins in the blood. We couldn't take an aspirin or eat without fear of life threatening effects.

What is cleansing or detox? The words are heard frequently in the news. Intuitively, we all know the importance of cleansing. Without the knowledge of formal practice, we manage our lives around our body's ability to cleanse with small changes in diet and physical exertion based on how we feel, or increase our bad behaviors in a blind attempt to feel better.

In natural healing, cleansing, detoxification, and detox are words with the same meaning, and I will use them interchangeably. Generally, cleansing is the removal of harmful wastes and toxins from the body. By removing toxic compounds, our body becomes more efficient and better able to heal and reverse disease.

Cleansing also refers to a large group of very diverse natural healing practices. It can refer to detoxifying deep tissues, the colon, blood, the lymphatic system, the kidneys and liver/gallbladder. It also refers to a wide variety of different treatment methods that include fasting, juice fasting, health retreats, mud wraps, bodywork techniques, herbal detoxification formulas, colonics, enemas, strict diets and many other

4

modalities. With so many variations, you can see why many Americans are confused about what cleansing is and how to best approach it.

For years I have seen patients, often filled with frustration, ask why they have a disease and what factors caused it. My experience and research have shown that toxins can either worsen or be a trigger for almost any disease process. Cleansing is one of the best ways to remove toxins and regain our health. The air we breathe, our land, our rivers, our homes, our furniture, the water we drink, the food we eat and even the clothes we wear are filled with toxins. It is my opinion that everyone living on Earth is exposed to toxins daily.

Health, radiant vitality and happiness are our birthrights. However, most doctors today don't realize we can have all of this for our entire lifespan. Western healthcare doesn't emphasize vibrant health and vitality because it only focuses on treating symptoms. Pharmacological drugs causes suppression of symptoms, and that does not lead to healing; it masks the disease process. Alternative medicine is based on treating the root causes of disease.

Cleansing conjures up images that range from taking gross tasting syrups, choking down thick, slimy fiber drinks, going on starvation diets and sitting on the toilet with severe bowel movements. Many cleansing practices are, in fact, extremely unhealthy. Even though they are natural, they are not necessarily healthy. I have seen many patients get worse from doing cleanses that were not suited for their particular constitution or illness.

And there are simply cleanses that might not cause benefit. There is, for example, a small, renowned group of monks who live in Belgium. For years, they have followed what I personally believe to be of the most distinct health cleanses on Earth. In addition to being an essential spiritual service to their community, this monastery also produces the famous Chimmay brand beers. Considered to be of the best in the world, if you have an interest in trying them you can feel good knowing that each bottle is blessed. Once a year, for seven straight days, they eat nothing and only drink beer.

I'm not criticizing the monks. And to be fair this is the only cleanse I have encountered but not tried. But it does illuminate my concern about cleansing programs that may not cause benefits towards one's health.

HOLISTIC CLEANSING

Holistic cleansing is a process of whole body rejuvenation and detox that embraces lifestyle modification, emotional transformation, positive affirmation, dietary change, specific herbal supplements and spiritual growth. It involves following a complete program and regime over a specified amount of time with a clear goal. It is not just one single activity and can assist anyone in achieving balance and vibrant health. Holistic means, in essence, to embrace the whole of who we are and where we are going. Holistic cleansing is much more than just pooping or peeing all day!

Holistic cleansing allows you to heal your body, eliminate harmful toxins, balance your emotions and regain your sense of spiritual well being. It provides a stimulus to create a new life and reach new levels of feeling healthy.

You are not doing a holistic cleanse if you put your feet in some detoxifying foot bath, go to a health food store and buy a liver cleansing product or spend all day sitting in a sauna sweating out toxins. A holistic cleanse is a wonderful and beautiful system to purge the body of all toxins and rejuvenate every cell of our bodies. It is one of the most empowering and transforming experiences a person can go through.

I grew up in an agricultural town in Nebraska and as such I am inclined to use nature analogies. A good holistic cleanse is like farming. Farmers need to have a clear goal and the knowledge to successfully achieve it. They must know the seasons of nature and the right time of year to plant seeds. They must tend to their crops in just the right way or they will not grow to be bountiful. A farmer must also know when to harvest, otherwise his hard work is for nothing. And a good farmer knows when to rest.

Holistic cleansing has a proper time and season. Like the farmer, one needs to know when to rest or take breaks from cleansing. The cleanse itself is our labor; we have to make sure we are following our regime of diet, supplements and other lifestyle changes. It is the planting of seeds that will grow into the rewards of our efforts. The harvest of cleansing is the numerous health rewards from properly finishing. If everything is done right, you will all have a surplus of health.

CHAPTER TWO

THE HISTORY OF CLEANSING & DETOX

There are few time-honored traditions in existence today as important as seasonal cleansing. Cleansing has been a vital part of health maintenance programs practiced by almost every culture on every continent for over a thousand years. People often wonder why cultures as diverse as German, Egyptian, Indian, and South American value seasonal cleanses. The answer is simple. It is the foundation of a healthy body and mind.

Traditionally, in European northern climates, seasonal cleanses were most often used to help purge the body of excess toxins and alleviate digestive problems from the heavy meals eaten during the winter months. These dense and congestive meals in combination with less exercise create a deep stagnation in the tissues of the body. Cleansing has always been the best way to stimulate the body's innate system of renewal. Numerous religious traditions also used cleansing and fasting to reach new levels of meditation, prayer and insight. In fact, not long ago in Europe, monks and priests were *the only herbalists*. They served as healers, maintained active herbal medicine gardens and practiced countless types of cleansing techniques for all those in need. Natural healing was considered a sacred profession, and priests and monks were also often healers because they were of the few who could read. Many of the world's time honored religious ceremonies still incorporate elements of these older cleansing practices.

ANCIENT

The Egyptian documents known as the Papyrus Ebers are of the earliest known writing and were written circa 1550 B.C. Their focus is on medicine and natural healing. Specifically, they mention many cleansing herbs such as aloe, wormwood and senna. The Papyrus Ebers also mention other cleansing methods such as enemas.

As Greek culture rose to power, physicians began to further advance the practice of medicine and healing. In the fifth century B.C., the father of modern medicine, Hippocrates, wrote "Corpus Hippocraticum". It details many herbal medicines still used in contemporary herbalism. Much more information was further developed by the Romans and they subsequently spread their knowledge throughout Europe.

EUROPEAN

In Europe today, there are many different forms of cleansing, fasting and spa therapies. Many of the dietary fasting and cleansing programs typically reflect a variety of seasonal foods and diverse customs that are unique to each area. They often embrace local plants or local natural features such as warm springs. Cleansing therapies remains a time honored healing practice that still plays an important role in European medical systems. These treatments are often covered by insurance plans, and it is common to receive a recommendation from a medical doctor to go to a health spa for a week or two. Some of these spa towns are on healing springs that have been used for over a thousand years. Many of these were sites that played important roles during major wars since generals wanted their soldiers to be able to rejuvenate and recover before returning to battle.

European medical health spas have doctors who put patients on a variety of treatments including juice or broth fasts, cleansing herbal teas, massage, saunas, exercise, stretching, enemas, healing springs, mineral waters and nature walks. Some medical doctors specialize in these cleansing treatments. There is much more research done on the medical effects of cleansing spas in Europe than in America. Unfortunately, much of the research has not been translated into English.

Throughout most of Europe, these practices are so old and common that people often refer to these programs simply as "Fasting Cure,"

"Cleansing Cure" or "Spring Cure." I once asked a German herbalist why these programs were referred to as such. He emphatically replied, "Because cleansing can cure or help almost any disease."

AMERICAN

Just as the first medical training programs in America were based on the European model, most of our historical information on cleansing comes from Europe. Most Americans are surprised to learn that herbal medicine doctors have been a rich part of our history and culture. During different periods, these natural doctors represented many schools of thought and were known as Thomasonians, Physiomedicalists, Medical Botanists, and Eclectics. Their numbers once rivaled medical doctors and they treated life threatening medical conditions in their own clinics and hospitals.

The Eclectics were the last and most powerful. Their understanding of herbal medicine was advanced, and their clinical expertise was so successful that many contemporary herbalists are turning to their writings to regain information that has been lost. The Eclectics progressed the use of cleansing and detoxifying herbs beyond their European ancestors. They created volumes of books about the medical effects of cleansing herbs and fasting on curing many diseases.

Eli Jones and Dr. John Scudder were two of the most famous. Jones specialized in treating cancer with a group of herbs called alteratives. He created the famous "Compound of Scrophularia" that is still used in the natural treatment of many types of cancer. Dr. Scudder was an esteemed physician and teacher of Eclectic medicine. He created the famous "Scudder's Alterative" for use in detox programs and to help treat a variety of chronic diseases. The rise of the American Medical Association created a downward spiral of events that made it slowly illegal for these doctors to practice. Today, the Food and Drug Administration puts pressure on natural healing practitioners and supplement manufacturers from making any claims even when science backs them. They are either hostile towards these therapies or simply too passive or unwilling to admit their benefit. Can you imagine what the FDA would say if you advertised a "Cleansing Cure" here in the US?

NATIVE AMERICAN

Perhaps no other culture to exist on Earth lived closer in harmony with nature than Native Americans. Fasting and cleansing is not only part of their culture, it is also part of their spiritual rituals. It was – and still is – considered the best way to honor your connection to the creator by showing personal sacrifice. Fasting and cleansing programs are utilized before beginning any major ceremony. These ceremonies include vision quests, honoring the death of a loved one, healing rituals, sun dance ceremonies, seasonal changes, planetary/cosmic changes, harvest events, special hunts and anytime the favor of the divine is needed. I once asked the medicine man Pete Peterson (known as Medicine Eagle) why Native Americans valued fasting so much. He responded that fasting is one of the few ways to show the Great Mystery we are truly making a sacrifice because our bodies are the only thing we own. Money, cars, houses and land don't belong to us. How can we sacrifice something that doesn't belong to us? He continued by saying that fasting is the best way to create a highly attuned state to connect to our spiritual selves.

TRADITIONAL CHINESE MEDICINE

Traditional Chinese Medicine (TCM) is the native healing practice of China. At well over 2,500 years old, it is one of the oldest systems of medicine still in practice today. (Some scholars debate that it is more than 5000 years old.) It is practiced in every industrialized nation. Based on a very complex understanding of the body, its internal processes and how seasonal changes affect our health, TCM is a very exacting medical system that diagnoses complicated health problems. It understands each person's unique biorhythms, how emotions affect health and how to regain wellness.

Many people are surprised to know there is an ancient Chinese system of fasting called bigu or Pi Ku. Bigu cleansing diets are first mentioned back as far as the Qin dynasty. Bigu translates as "without grain" because one only eats fresh fruits and vegetables. No beans, rice, wheat or other grain is allowed. Advanced practitioners often go to more extremes of only drinking water for a specified peroid of time. This ancient practice is often called the "three worm diet" because it is thought worms or parasties live on grains.

This simple practice of bigu fasting is used by practitioners of martial arts and other Chinese spiritual healing masters during their training. Often patients are recommended to follow a bigu diet for seven days or longer to help heal. It well documented that many healing masters of ancient China went years on a bigu diet to cultivate their connection with nature.

Traditional Ayurvedic Medicine

No other cleansing healing system is quite as complex as Traditional Ayurvedic Medicine (TAM). Ayurveda is the traditional healing system of India. Like TCM, it is estimated to be at least 2,500 years old. It has an amazing time-tested intense method of whole body detox called Pancha Karma.

Pancha Karma is an entire series of practices that are performed anywhere from three to sixty-five days in a row. It combines a cleansing diet, fasting, hot oil massages, herbal enemas, detoxifying herbal supplements, yoga, breathing exercises, skin brushing, shirodhara (hot oil forehead massage) and many other optional modalities. In reality, it is the first truly comprehensive holistic detox practice in the world. Pancha Karma is usually done in a spa-like setting, where people check in for an entire length of treatment. There are no TVs, radios or phones. The entire focus is on healing, peace and rejuvenation.

Although pancha karma is the most complex system of detox, it is not accessible to most Americans. There are very few authentic practitioners performing it in America. It is also a very expensive treatment, often costing thousands of dollars. The Four Winds Holistic Cleanse was created to embrace many of these cleansing spa treatments used in pancha karma but in a much more affordable way. Many of these treatments can be performed at home at virtually no cost.

The Four Winds Holistic Cleanse embraces and draws on all the diverse wisdom of these time tested practices. By combining the accumulated experiences of our ancestors with the clinical practices and the latest modern research on natural medicine, a truly powerful system of cleansing is created. Since every person is truly unique, it takes a comprehensive program like the Four Winds Holistic Cleanse to safely meet the needs of Americans living in todays toxin filled world.

CHAPTER THREE

OVERVIEW OF CLEANSING ORGANS IN DETOX & HEALTH

There is an old saying that, "You are what you eat." Those of us in the nutrition world have a more accurate – albeit less flashy – saying. "You are only what you digest and assimilate." You can eat healthy food forever and take every prescription medication, but good health simply depends on what you break down, digest and assimilate. One needs to have a basic understanding of how the body's internal organs detoxify on a daily basis before truly understanding cleansing practices. Each organ of detox plays a vital role in removing certain toxins.

THE LIVER

Whenever we have a build up of toxins in our body, the liver is unable to function optimally and it becomes stressed. Just looking at the functions of the liver, one can begin to see why people feel terrible when they are toxic. The liver is of the most important organs of detox. It has the role of breaking down almost everything you put in your body – food, vitamins, medications, any liquid you drink, every food additive and much more. Many of the amazing functions of the liver are listed below:

Regulates the Digestive System The liver also secretes digestive enzymes that aid in the process of absorbing nutrients, and helps break down and assimilate carbohydrates, proteins and fats. This is why many people on high fat or high protein diets put stress on their liver.

Produces Bile Along with the gallbladder, the liver secretes bile, a gross, blackish-green fluid. It is one of the main stimulators of bowel movements and motility. A healthy liver is essential for regular bowel movements. As it is one of the body's major methods of breaking down cholesterol, many people with high cholesterol simply need a liver supporting diet and herbal supplements. As for its necessity, people who have their gallbladders removed frequently have continual or chronic troubles with digestion after surgery.

Detoxifies and Filters Chemicals in the Blood Detox is the most important function of the liver. Almost every single thing eaten, breathed or put on the skin has to be processed or broken down by the body. The liver has to constantly monitor everything in the bloodstream, labeling it as friend or foe. This process is happening every second of our lives and is necessary for survival of the human body. We would die very quickly if our liver could not detoxify and filter blood. This is one of the countless examples that demonstrate the inherent wisdom and healing power of the body.

Assists the Nervous System The liver helps regulate many neurotransmitters that control emotional and psychological health. Many Americans are surprised to discover that the liver helps regulate levels of many neurotransmitters, including seratonin. You can quickly begin to see why liver cleanses can have a dramatic impact on your mood and happiness.

Regulates Hormone Levels and Assists in Hormone Synthesis The liver does it all! It constantly monitors levels of circulating hormones in the body. Sometimes it directly causes their metabolism or breakdown. Other times it sends signals to other bodily command centers to increase or decrease secretion of hormones.

Other Assorted Functions A few other functions of importance include the building of proteins, maintaining fluid balance, monitoring electrolyte levels and storing excess blood in cases of emergencies. The liver also oversees the production of many immune system chemicals, thereby contributing to our overall health.

MEDICAL MODEL OF THE LIVER

Western science describes the liver as a virtual chemical factory of the body. It is known to be involved in more than 500 vital bodily processes. It is easy to understand the importance of the liver in cleansing because it serves as a filter for everything circulating in the blood. It has to break down hormones (testosterone, estrogen, etc.), detoxify water and fat based soluble chemicals (including drugs, medications, pesticides, etc.) and neutralize toxins. The liver even stores necessary vitamins and minerals. Unfortunately, it also stores excess toxins the body cannot breakdown.

CLASSICAL CHINESE CONCEPT OF THE LIVER AND ITS FUNCTIONS

In Traditional Chinese Medicine, the liver and gallbladder are seen from a more holistic viewpoint. The functions of the liver are to regulate the flow of chi (vital life force) throughout the body, stimulate the circulation of blood and assist in the building of strong blood, regulate digestion and promote normal bowel movements, regulate hormones and to create harmony of the emotions. Emotions of anger and frustration are often seen as "hot" or "stagnant" liver imbalances. The liver is eloquently described as "the general of the body," to stress how it is the active organizing force. There is an old Chinese saying that, "When the liver is balanced, one should feel like a free and easy wander."

KIDNEYS

The kidneys play many roles in cleansing and detox. Together with the liver, they help to filter impurities from the blood. The liver itself helps to make many toxins water soluble so they can be flushed out by the kidneys and bladder by urination. The kidneys also play a role in preventing poisons, acids and toxins from accumulating in the body. Many toxins in our environment also can be stored in the kidneys and gradually have a negative influence on their function over time. Heavy metal toxins in our diet and drinking water are known to cause damage to the kidneys over time. This is why people may experience mild lower backaches, increased urination and foul smelling urine when detoxifying.

CLASSICAL CHINESE CONCEPT OF THE KIDNEYS

In TCM, the Kidneys are called "the doorway of life and death." That statement shows how much emphasis is placed on their health. They control many functions including the balance of yin and yang, assisting building strong bones, the growth of hair, all reproductive functions, regulating vitality and are directly associated with longevity. The kidneys are associated closely with the adrenals and entire endocrine (hormonal) system. The emotions of fear, worry and paranoia are signs of kidney imbalance.

LYMPHATIC SYSTEM

Unless you are a massage therapist or have cancer, most people have never heard of the lymphatic system. It is a small network of vessels that run alongside many of our veins and arteries. It is the house of our immune system. It is the area where the body creates the response to an infection. This is why any time we are sick, we often first have swollen lymph glands in the neck. The lymphatic system is also a major source of detoxification in the body because it moves fluids into and out of the deeper tissues of the body. The lymph vessels also transport many fats, oils and some toxins. Many natural health experts feel lymphatic system health is one of the most important factors in preventing tumors. When it becomes congested, the body is more prone to form ovarian cysts, breast cysts, boils and cancerous tumors.

LYMPHATIC HOME SELF TEST

Wondering if your lymphatic system is congested? There are two easy ways to make this determination. One, feel the areas under the neck and chin, if they are swollen, tender or painful, you likely have some lymphatic stagnation. Two, vigorously pound your chest (like Tarzan) over your heart for about 10 seconds. When you stop, you should feel an intense buzzing or vibration in the area where your heart is. This is your thymus gland, the master gland of the lymphatic system and the entire immune system. If you do not feel buzzing, it is usually a sign your lymphatic system is congested.

LARGE AND SMALL INTESTINE

Anytime you mention cleansing, most people first think of laxatives and uncomfortable diarrhea. As you have already seen, this is not the case. The intestines control about 25% of the body's detox functions, and their primary function is to absorb nutrients. Many beneficial bacteria are contained in the intestinal lining. The role of these bacteria is to secret enzymes that transform numerous types of toxins into substances that can be released from the body. The intestines also release fat-soluble toxins in the bile by bowel movements. When the intestines are toxic and people are chronically constipated, the body slowly reabsorbs these toxins into the blood stream. Any good holistic cleansing program should promote bowel regularity. It is important to note that constipation during a cleanse is a bad sign. With constipation, all the toxins that are dumped into the intestines will be reabsorbed into the bloodstream and an extra burden will be placed on the liver. Intestinal reabsorbtion of toxins can make people extremely sick.

SKIN

Did you know the skin is the largest organ of the body? Did you know the skin is a major organ of detox? The body uses the skin to push out toxins from deep in the tissues and the lymphatic system. Many fat-soluble toxins – such as some pesticides and heavy metals – are excreted through sweat. I recall a patient who worked in a metal processing plant. Every time he came in, I could smell the metallic-like odor of his body. Have you ever had that healing sweat from breaking a fever and have your loved one say, "You stink!" That is your body's natural detox process at work. There are a series of glands under the skin, called sebaceous glands, that are stimulated by sweating. This is why acne, pimples, boils, cysts and funky smelling sweat are all common signs to start a cleanse. As another detox self-test, examine your shirts in the closet. If you have foul smelling sweat or lots of sweat stains on your shirts, then your lymphatic system and skin most likely need help detoxifying.

Deep Tissues

I saved the best for last – the deep tissues are a vital part of cleansing. However, they are almost always misunderstood or overlooked. The deep tissues simply refer to everything in the body that is not an organ. It is the layer of fluids that surround each organ and all the 'gooey mess" of the body. It is a big wet swamp. The deep tissues are those murky areas (called interstitial spaces in western medicine) between all the organs where most metabolism and transfer of toxins happen. It is where much of the action and communication of the body takes place. Even though they are not the organs themselves, the deep tissues influence every organ and cell. It is my clinical opinion that the deep tissues play a key role in stimulating new cell growth.

Almost all cleanses in America today don't address the deep tissues. One needs to not only change the metabolic state of all the organs, but also the deep tissues stimulation. Without deep tissus stimulation, a cleanse is superficial. In a nutshell, a cleanse is not really "deeply" affecting the body unless the deep tissues are detoxified.

Detox On a Scientific Note

Let's take a more technical look at the body's detox processes. The liver detoxifies or deactivates virtually every chemical in the bloodstream. This is usually achieved by a number of mechanisms. These natural detoxifying liver compounds are part of what is called the microsomal enzyme system, an extremely complex system by which the liver detoxifies dangerous chemicals via various enzymes. It can be broken down into two general categories, Phase I and Phase II enzymes of detoxification. Below is a brief "nutshell" scientific description of how the liver detoxifies for you researchers and scientists out there:

- *Kupffer Cells* break down antibodies, bacteria and immune cells.

- *Bile* breaks down cholesterol, fat soluble toxins and numerous chemicals.

- *Phase I Enzymes* are one of the two major pathways the liver detoxifies. They help detoxify environmental toxins, alcohol, almost all prescription drugs, caffeine, histamine, food dyes, most non-prescription drugs, some toxic acids, insecticides, nicotine, hormones, inflammation chemicals, bowel toxins, metabolites, and many other chemicals. The liver achieves this through an enzyme called cytochrome P450. Basically this enzyme directly neutralizes chemicals by making them water-soluble and converting them into a less toxic chemical. Cytochrome P450 enzyme can also modify these harmful chemicals into an even more toxic substance that can be more easily recognized by Phase II enzymes. The basic key is that cytochrome P450 alters foreign substances into a compound our livers can more effectively detoxify.

- *Phase II Enzymes* are the second major process. In Phase II, a variety of different enzymes conjugate (meaning to attach chemicals to) toxins. This process makes them easier for the liver and kidneys to detoxify. Many chemicals are neutralized this way, including the following: aspirin, carcinogens, some hormones, some neurotransmitters, fat soluble chemicals not removed by bile, blood thinning medications, acetaminophen and many other toxins. The key concept is that enzymes and glucuronic acid remove toxins by a process called conjugation. Conjugation occurs when protective chemicals are added to the toxin so it can be excreted safely. There are many enzymes that play a role in phase II detox, including glutathione. This is the main mechanism the body detoxifies carcinogens (cancerous causing chemicals). Many cleansing supplements increase glutathione levels. Elevated glutathione levels prevents cellular and genetic damage.

Research has shown that even a single food or group of food can stimulate liver detox. Phenethyl isothiocyanate (PEITC), a compound stimulated by the intake of watercress, has been shown to induce the liver's Phase II detoxification enzymes. PEITC has been shown to inhibit the spread of cancer cells, inhibit the production of tumors and trigger cancer cell death. It has also been shown to reverse dangerous inflammatory compounds that are linked to cancer.

The scientific basis of cleansing is growing daily. We now know that cruciferous vegetables (such as broccoli, brussel sprouts, cauliflower and watercress) have powerful anticancer effects. These power foods contain phytochemicals called glucosinolates. The body converts or hydrolyzes these into chemicals called isothiocyanates. Isothiocyanates are powerful chemicals that have been shown to counter breast, lung, colon, head, neck and prostate cancers.

CHAPTER FOUR

WHAT IS A TOXIN?

"What befalls the Earth, befalls the children of the Earth."
Chief Seattle

We are constantly bombarded by the word "toxin." Psychologists use it to refer to a "toxic environment" or "toxic person" in one's life. Researchers use the word to refer to a wide variety of chemical compounds that can trigger diseases in our bodies. Natural healers refer to it when describing the amazing amount of destructive forces, pesticides, food additives and chemicals that our bodies have to deal with on a daily basis. Spiritualists can refer to toxins as negative thoughts that cause us to do things that destroy our spiritual grace. Herbalists classically describe a toxin as potentially harmful to the body either as a byproduct of metabolism or from an exogenous (from outside the body) compound. Environmentalists refer to toxins in regard to persistent chemicals that negatively affect nature in some way – on algae, the ozone layers, water quality and numerous other areas. Can everyone be right? In this case, yes.

A toxin must be thought of in a very comprehensive way that can integrate all of these valid insights from a wide variety of health perspectives. A toxin is anything in our environment that our bodies have to deal with in order to maintain a state of homeostatic balance. Homeostatic balance is the body's innate ability to protect its own health.

HOLISTIC DEFINITION OF A TOXIN

The wisdom of Traditional Chinese Medicine (TCM) loosely defines a toxin as "anything that prevents us from attaining perfect, radiant health." Anything that prevents us from attaining emotional happiness, spiritual fulfillment, homeostatic balance and our highest state of physical health is a toxin. Anything that impairs the body's innate wisdom and ability to heal itself or any substance that can trigger the disease process is also a toxin.

Holistic cleansing is so vital because we need to understand our weaknesses on all levels (including body, spirit, mind, environment and living conditions) before we can create an effective plan for regaining our health. Hopefully, in the process of cleansing, lifelong healthy habits are created.

Five years ago, I thought we could easily minimize our exposure to toxins in our lives by drinking pure water, eating organic food, reducing the use of synthetic medications, using natural farming methods, avoiding pesticides, using natural household cleaners and focusing on being relaxed. As more and more research has accumulated, I have totally changed my understanding. I now believe with clear scientific support that everyone on Earth is challenged by different toxins. Cleansing has now become necessary for any person who is interested in being healthy. If you live in a monastery, you are surrounded by toxins. If you live deep in the woods, you are surrounded by toxins. My deepest hope with this book is that it will inspire everyone to begin living a more all natural, "green" lifestyle for our health, Earth, children and future generations.

There are thousands of toxins in our lives today. In fact, it is part of everyday living because we have supported the corporations that create new chemicals for our needs and desires. Excluding the rest of the world, the EPA estimates between 1700 and 2000 new compounds are introduced every year in America. To approve a new chemical, the government only requires safety tests on human health if there is pre-existing evidence of potential harm. EPA test records show that only about 25% of the 82,000 chemicals we use in the US have ever been researched for toxicity. No one, at this point in time, can trust the government and its limited resources to ensure the safety of these chemical toxins. In today's world of corporate power, you can be assured that few of these new man made chemicals are tested for safety. For example, in October 2007, the EPA approved a highly toxic chemical pesticide called methyl iodide to be used in strawberry and tomato farms. Five Nobel laureates and 49 scientists protested because the chemical is a known neurotoxin and carcinogen that can seep into groundwater.

In a new study released by the Environmental Working Group (EWG), researchers tested umbilical cord blood of babies born in the US. Their test showed a shocking total of 287 chemical toxins in the umbilical cords of newborns. The average per baby was found to be about 200 different industrial chemicals and pollutants. Of the chemicals found, 180 are known to cause cancer and 217 are known to be toxic to the brain and nervous system. One of the oddest chemicals found is one that is used to manufacture Teflon non-stick pans. The absolutely worst aspect is that these are newborns.

Medical doctors often think cleansing is not an important topic, but this study clearly shows holistic detox therapies may be the only way we have to counteract this mess. You can further safeguard your health by being educated on the sources of these toxins and try to limit your exposure to them. I could write an entire book on toxins, so I will keep it generalized. I highly encourage anyone to research this area more by checking the resource section which includes the EWG website.

COMMON TOXINS MOST AMERICANS ENCOUNTER

Food additives, artificial coloring, artificial flavorings, artificial
    sweeteners and food preservatives
Genetically modified foods
Contaminated Seafood (mercury)
Foods high in synthetic hormones (milk, animal meats, etc.)
Hydrogenated oils and rancid fats
Stimulants (caffeine, ephedrine, etc.)
Cigarette smoke
All illegal drugs
Contaminated drinking water (heavy metals, pesticides, etc.)
Many over the counter (OTC) and prescription medications
Some vaccinations
Chronic stress

Chronic emotional states (such as depression, anxiety, anger, fear, worry, frustration)

Cleaning chemicals

Nonstick and stain-resistant cookware (perfluorinated acids)

Many cosmetics (lead, heavy metals)

Fragrances in shampoos and soaps (phthalates)

Many colognes and perfumes

Household paints

New furniture (fire retardant compounds like PBDEs, glues, etc.)

New carpet (glues, fire retardant compounds, etc.)

Pesticides and fertilizers

Environmental pollutants (air, water and ground)

Toxic vapors, toxic gases and air pollution

Industrial chemicals (dioxins, etc.)

Smog, car and airplane exhaust

Numerous synthetic chemicals

Heavy metals (mercury, arsenic, lead, etc.)

Plastic bottles and containers (xenoestrogens, bisphenol A, etc.)

That covers just about all areas of life! Even our car interiors, house paints and plastic bottles we drink from are sources of toxins. One can easily see why there is a growing awareness about living a natural lifestyle. There are many things we can do to become more "green" such as drinking purified water, eliminating toxic lawn chemicals and using all natural household cleaners. There are hundreds of easy changes that can be made. It is exciting that we can make most of these all natural products at home. People are empowered to know they can save money, become more self-sufficient and healthier by making many of these "green" changes.

When we look at the sheer amount of toxins in our daily life, it is easy to see why many consider the role of cleansing to be vital for health. That is why many of the lifestyle recommendations discussed in later chapters are vital to follow. A strict organic cleansing diet can be followed, but the effectiveness of the cleanse can be limited if synthetic shampoos, bug sprays and lawn chemicals are still used. Holistic cleansing causes us to reexamine our entire lifestyle.

For many years scientists argued that we couldn't prove toxins affected our health. Now, despite fierce opposition from corporations, scientists are beginning to study the devastating effects of many of these chemicals on our bodies and the environment. There are now a small number of labs worldwide that can test blood and urine for a number of these environmental toxins. A few labs are running tests that can measure up to 320 different toxins in the body. With easily over 80,000 in the United States, this is only a first step. Unfortunately, most doctors aren't aware of these tests, and they are currently extremely expensive. In 2006, each cost between $10,000 and $15,000. It is my prediction and hope that toxin testing will someday become a common part of our healthcare system. More medical doctors and naturopaths are currently testing for heavy metals. Scientists are also starting to measure the amounts of specific pollutants, pharmaceuticals and toxic waste in our local environments.

Here are a few recent examples of reported statistics:

- The World Health Organization estimates about three million cases of pesticide poisoning occur worldwide each year.

- Environmentalists estimate over fifty ocean "dead zones" off the US coast alone. These are areas so polluted with toxic chemicals that no aquatic life can grow.

- Many rivers in the US are testing positive for anti-depressant medications, estrogens, chemical fertilizers, toxic metals, farming fertilizer, insecticide runoff and other prescription meds. The most alarming aspect is that sewage treatment plants aren't designed to remove most pharmaceuticals and toxins. Whatever we flush down the toilet or pour in the sewers may be in trace amounts of our drinking water.

- Sierra Magazine reported a recent test on cosmetics in the US and found many common products have over 200 known toxins, including lead.

- The American Cancer Society states that an estimated 75-80% of cancers are due to exposure to environmental carcinogens and only 5-10% of cancers are inherited.

- A study in the New England Journal of Medicine reported that for every 10-unit increase in pollution, a woman's risk of dying from heart disease rose by about 75%.

- The Earth Day Organization reported that an average of 1 million American children eat 15 or more pesticides daily on fruits and vegetables.

- A study by the Natural Resource Defense Council (NRDC) found lead, pathogens, trihalomethanes, rocket fuel and arsenic in the drinking water of 19 major US cities. The EPA estimates one in five Americans consume tap water that does not meet the Safe Water Drinking Act Standards.

- An EWG survey found that the average adult is exposed to 126 chemicals every day, just in their personal care products alone.

- Another EWG study reported that one in every thirteen women is exposed to a known human carcinogen every day.

THE STORY OF BISPHENOL A

Bisphenol A (BPA) is a synthetic chemical used to manufacture plastic containers, baby bottles, toys, dental sealants, flame-retardants and many other plastic goods. It acts similarly to estrogen in the body. In 2003, about 13 billion kilograms were manufactured, making it one of the most common synthetic chemicals produced. The bad news is BPA leaches out of plastic bottles into liquids and is absorbed in the human digestive tract. I must stress that my biggest concern is that BPA is used in baby milk bottles. Scientists have recently linked BPA with a number of health problems including infertility, obesity, sperm abnormalities, miscarriages, breast and prostate cancers, brain development in children, and possibly some birth defects. In 2005, the Centers for Disease Control and Prevention found Bisphenol A in the urine of 95% of people tested.

While drinking distilled water is an important change for overall health, it is undermined by being stored in plastic bottles, another source of added toxins. Cleansing is the only way to counteract the hundreds of daily toxins we ingest.

GENETICALLY MODIFIED FOODS (GMOS)

Genetically Modified Foods (GMOs) are also a known toxin. They should be avoided at all cost, because there is little to no research on them at this time. The only way to gaurante a product in not genetically altered is to buy certified organic food. At this time, certified organic foods are safe (for now). The words of Phil Angell, Director of Corporate Communication for Monsanto sums up the mindset of corporate America. An October 25th, 1998 article in the New York Times quotes him as saying, "Monsanto should not have to vouchsafe the safety of biotech food, our interest is in selling as much of it as possible. Assuring the safety is the FDA's job."

CHAPTER FIVE

HERBAL MEDICINES: NATURE'S GIFTS OF HEALING

"Those who do not know plants could never accurately judge their virtues."

CAROLUS LINNAEUS, SWEDISH PHYSICIAN
AND FATHER OF BOTANY, 1707-1778

Herbal medicine is the most ancient and continually practiced form of healing on the planet. As long as humans have been alive, we have used herbs as food, medicine and ways to connect to the divine. The World Health Organization states that herbal medicine is still currently used as a primary source of medicine for over 80% of the world's population. There are records of herbal medicine going back 10,000 years! One of the most astonishing facts from new research by anthropologists is that primates and other animals have a working knowledge of about 10-25 medicinal herbs. They commonly treat each other for illnesses like infections and parasites. This is not surprising to Native American medicine men/women because many of their ancient teachings tell of their ancestors first learning about herbal medicines by observing animals in nature. Research is starting to show that our own DNA co-evolved together with plants. In many ways, humans are genetically programmed to utilize and understand herbal medicines.

Like the ancient Native Americans taught, we as a people and culture are beginning to understand that every plant on earth has a purpose as well as a healing and medicinal quality.

Demystifying Alterative Herbs

Alteratives are a major category of herbal remedies that have been used throughout history by all cultures. These herbs affect detox throughout the entire body and even in the organs themselves. They are the most important herbs to affect metabolism and stimulate change in the deep tissues. The old American herbal doctors called alteratives "blood purifiers," a term many clinical herbalists still use today. I personally feel this is one of the most descriptive and accurate definitions.

One of my teachers described it best when he said that alteratives alter or change the state of the tissues of the body. They cause old diseased tissues to be removed and new healthy tissues to be stimulated to grow. They are so exciting because they allow us to actually alter our entire body into something new and healthy. How empowering is that? They are one of the main ways to stimulate your entire body to rapidly restore itself.

Clearly Defining an Alterative

Cleansing herbs help the liver to filter, excrete, detoxify and safely modify many of the toxins that are constantly circulating in our blood. But while many herbs are cleansing, few can be classified as alterative. As such, there is much confusion and heated debate regarding what an alterative is in the alternative medicine profession. Based on my own research and clinical experience, I have created my own insights on what characteristics define them:

ONE

Alteratives increase elimination of metabolic waste via detoxifying organs of the body. All alteratives stimulate detoxification in the body. The liver, kidneys and lymphatic system are most commonly affected.

TWO

All alterative herbs create increased activity in the deep tissues of the body. They actually improve the state and health of the deep tissues in two ways. One, through detox processes in the organs and cells. Two, by increasing the movement of exchange through interstitial spaces of the body. In general, they help eliminate stagnation of fluids deep in the tissues. In essence, the deep tissues are all those areas between organs (called interstitial spaces) where most the exchange of nutrients and toxins takes place.

THREE

Alteratives cause a change in human biological metabolism to a more catabolic state. When the body is in a catabolic state, it is in a state of breakdown (or detox). This brings up the vital point that cleansing is a largely catabolic process. What happens over time is the body breaks down diseased tissues and eliminates waste. In essence, alteratives direct bodily resources to "burn off" toxins and old products of bad metabolism. In my opinion, alteratives can direct the breakdown of disease triggering compounds from genetic errors such as cancer triggering compounds. This is similar to what happens during an infection. Our body "burns off" old immune cells and viral/bacterial compounds. This catabolic nature is exactly why cleansing should only be done for short periods.

FOUR

When finished taking a round of alteratives, new tissues are stimulated to grow. The body's innate ability to heal and rejuvenate will be dramatically increased. New scientific research is starting to show that these herbs affect even our genes and help them direct the expression of the healing of diseases. When we are done with cleansing, our bodies then have an increased ability to rejuvenate new cells and tissues. A true alterative works even after you stop taking them. The same can not be said about prescription drugs.

What is very exciting is that alteratives have many other benefits than cleansing. They also have a variety of other highly beneficial properties such as antiviral, antibacterial, antimutagenic, antifungal, tumor inhibiting, anti-inflammatory, antioxidant, anticancer, hormone balancing, immune strengthening and other healing properties.

Alteratives are so powerful that we should usually only use them for short peroids of time. I want to restate one fact again. Alteratives and the cleansing process are both catabolic. If people cleanse for too long, it can lead to weight loss, fatigue, weakened immunity, muscle loss, and endocrine imbalance. I have seen hundreds of patients come in for appointments who had been doing a cleanse for months or even years. They weren't getting any better because they were breaking their body down without time to repair. Everyone should be reminded as to why we need to pay more attention to our lifestyle during a cleanse. It is because we are more susceptible to infections. This is also why we choose to use cleansing therapies with great care in weak patients, the elderly or those undergoing cancer treatments.

I include this following information to give the reader an understanding of how complex and how much planning go into creating a balanced detox system. To create a whole body detox, the supplement program uesd in the Four Winds Holistic Cleanse contains all the following types of herbal medicines.

Specific Herbs for Deep Tissue Cleansing

Let us examine some of the major herbs that stimulate detox. Besides alteratives, there are numerous other types of herbs that stimulate cleansing that we will briefly examine. For a cleanse to be complete, it should combine herbs from at least three of the following groups along with alteratives.

Bitter Herbs stimulate digestion, bile secretion, bowel motility and digestive enzyme production. They also increase the flow and secretion of liver enzymes, gently detoxify the liver and break down some hormones.

Angelica root	Artichoke leaf	Barberry root
Bitter Orange peel	Blue Vervain herb	Boldo herb
Calamus root*	Centaury herb	Dandelion root
Devil's Claw root	Gentian root	Hops flower
Juniper berry	Mugwort herb	Picorhizza herb
Prickly Ash bark	Quassia bark	Southernwood herb*
Wormwood herb*		Yarrow flower

Hepatic Herbs support the overall function and health of the liver, support mild liver detoxification, can help reverse liver damage, stimulate regeneration of liver cells, are good for long-term use and are also good to use after the cleanse is over to maintain liver function.

Blessed Thistle herb	Bupleurum root	Burdock root
Chicory root	Dandelion root	Milk Thistle seed
Oregon Grape root	Picorhizza herb	Toadflax herb
Watercress leaf		Yellow Dock root

Cholagogue Herbs cause the release and secretion of bile from the gallbladder, create deeper movement of toxins through the liver channels and ducts, help chronic constipation from a sluggish liver and are used to create a deeper action of liver cleansing herbs.

Artichoke leaf	Balmony herb	Barberry root
Celandine leaf*	Culvers root*	Fringetree bark
Mugwort leaf	Red Alder bark	Wahoo root*
White Popular bark		Wild Yam root

Alterative/Deep Cleanser/Blood Purifier Herbs create detoxification of the liver at its deepest levels, cleanse the deep tissues of the body, create movement of fluids in the deep tissues, have broad spectrum cleansing properties, cause the release/breakdown of diseased or old tissues, stimulate the growth of new tissues and are used to drive cleansing formulas into a deeper level of the body.

Black Alder bark	Blue Flag root*	Bupleurum root
Figwort root	Oregon Grape root	Red Alder root
Red Clover flower	Sarsaparilla root	Sassafras bark*
Stillingia root	Violet leaf	Yellow Dock root

Catalyst Herbs enhance the effects of the formula, drive the action of the formula deeper into the tissues and improve the taste or digestibility of a formula.

Ginger root	Cardamom seed	Licorice root
Lobelia herb*	Orange peel	Prickly Ash bark

Liver Restorative/Liver Protective/Liver Antioxidant Herbs are scientifically shown to regenerate and protect liver cells from toxins and possess potent antioxidant effects on supporting the normal function of the liver. Long-term usage is to maintain liver health by normalizing liver function. Most of these herbs have special applications for those with hepatitis and certain types of cancer treatments.

Artichoke leaf	Beet root	Eclipta root
Lyci berry	Milk Thistle seed	Reishi mushroom
Rosemary herb	Saffron petals	Schizandra berry
Shitake mushroom		Turmeric root

Laxative Herbs stimulate bowel movements and have a fairly strong cleansing action. It is always important to do a small amount of laxatives during a cleanse. If you are constipated or not having two bowel movements daily during a cleanse, you are reabsorbing toxins in your intestines. Laxatives can be habit forming if used for long periods of time including the herbs listed below. Unlike stronger herbal purgatives or drug store laxatives, these particular herbs all have many other specific cleansing actions.

Black Walnut hulls	Buckthorn bark	Cascara Sagrada bark
Butternut bark	Aloe Vera inner leaf	Rhubarb root

NOTE: We are not using attacking purgatives like senna, as these herbs only stimulate diarrhea but have little cleansing action.

Lymphatic Herbs create deep movement of lymphatic fluids around the organs of the body, assist with reduction/prevention of tumors, assist in filtering old immune cells, detoxify the entire lymphatic system and glands of the body, restore balance of the endocrine system, stimulate detox at deeper interstitial level, create movement in the sluggish deep tissues of the body and stimulate exchange of waste products and toxins from the glands.

Burdock root	Cleavers herb	Echinacea root
Figwort herb	Poke root*	Prickly Ash bark
Red Clover flower	Red root	Stillingia root
	Violet leaf	

Cleansing Diuretic Herbs stimulate the kidneys to detoxify, gently flush the kidneys, remove many acids from the body, stimulate the release of water soluble toxins, protect the kidneys during detox, have a mild alterative action on the kidneys themselves and restore kidney function.

Buchu leaf	Cleavers herb	Dandelion leaf
Gravel root	Juniper berry	Pippsissewia herb
Stillingia root	Parsley leaf	Uva Ursi leaf
	Celery root	

* These particular herbs are very strong and should only be used under the guidance of a naturopath or clinical herbalist.

ALTERATIVES AND THE SPECIFIC DETOX ORGANS THEY EFFECT

Organ	Specific Herbs for Detox
Liver	Milk Thistle seed, Yellow Dock root, Burdock root, Oregon Grape root, Turmeric root, Blessed Thistle herb
Large Intestine, Small Intestine	Cascara Sagrada bark, Buckthorn bark, Red Alder bark, Butternut bark, Black Walnut hulls
Kidney	Pipsissewia herb, Uva Ursi leaf, Dandelion leaf, Juniper berry, Stillingia herb, Hydrangea root
Lymphatic System	Red Clover flower, Cleavers herb, Figwort herb, Burdock root, Red Root root
Blood	Red Clover flower, Sarsaparillia root, Yellow Dock root, Oregon Grape root, Stillingia root, Figwort herb
Deep Tissues	Poke root, Red Clover flowers, Figwort herb, Stillingia root, Sarsarapilla root
Skin	Red Clover root, Cleavers herb, Figwort herb, Red Alder bark, Yellow Dock root, Oregon Grape root, Sarsaparilla root

CONSIDERATIONS WITH LAXATIVES

Laxatives have long been controversial among both western medical providers and natural healing experts. Some people praise their virtues while others feel even small doses will cause bowel dependency. Like all things, the truth lies somewhere in the middle. Herbal laxatives are much safer than prescriptions and over the counter drug store laxatives (many of which have known cancer risks). If constipation is a problem while cleansing, there are guidelines discussed for properly dosing laxatives in later chapters. They should only be used during the cleanse, in the minimum amount necessary and the formula should be very balanced and safe. Many herbalists feel that small amounts combined with other herbs in formulas such as ginger root will not cause bowel dependency. The collective wisdom of clinicians and most research shows that small amounts of these laxatives used during cleansing can actually strengthen bowel muscles and normal motility when used in moderate dosages.

An Important Point to Remember

Healing many chronic diseases will require other medical, lifestyle, dietary and natural healing treatments. A holistic cleanse is the key element to a comprehensive plan to overcome many diseases. Most patients notice their symptoms lessening after each cleanse. Patients should consult with a trained natural medicine practitioner if they want to incorporate other treatments or have questions about what to do between cleanses. The more of a natural lifestyle you can embrace, the more likely it is you will heal.

CHAPTER SIX

HEALING WITH THE SEASONS
– MAGIC WINDOWS

It is traditionally thought that just as in nature, each season represents a major physical and psychological change in our bodies. The seasons have played a major role in health and religious ceremony for thousands of years. This overlooked concept is vital to Traditional Chinese, Ayurvedic and Native American wisdom. Many current religious ceremonies once were associated with seasonal cleansing practices. Our bodies do expend a great deal of energy trying to adapt to each change in season and go through very precise and predictable changes. In the US, we practically live inside all day breathing in allergens, working under artificial light and using irritating chemicals. We may be oblivious to the season or weather because our office and home thermostats are set at a standard all year long, but nonetheless these changes still occur.

All cultures traditionally emphasize that each season is a "magic window" of healing. Certain organs and body systems are more active and receptive to healing in different seasons. Traditional Chinese and Ayurvedic medicine describe precisely how our bodies change with each season as they follow the rhythms of nature. Certain diseases will worsen or begin in certain seasons. I have found this information to be extremely valuable when working with patients who have mysterious or unknown medical conditions.

The basic concept is by changing our diet and taking detoxifying supplements with each season, the body more easily adapts or harmonizes with nature. A seasonal approach to cleansing also allows us to constantly focus on preventative health instead of trying to treat diseases once they start.

The following chart is based on TCM and my own experience with cleansing. The chart shows the organs which are most active each season and therefore the best to cleanse. Just a reminder, the Four Winds Holistic Cleanse targets all the internal organs and can be used in any season.

CHINESE FIVE PHASE SYSTEM AND THE SEASONS

Season	Element	Organ	Best Cleanse
Spring	Wood	Liver, Gallbladder	Liver, Gallbladder, Deep Tissues, Blood
Summer	Fire	Heart, Small Intestine, Pericardium, Triple Warmer	Small Intestine, Parasite
Indian Summer	Earth	Spleen, Pancreas, Stomach	None
Fall	Metal	Lung, Large Intestine	Large Intestine, Lymphatic Tissue, Deep Tissue
Winter	Water	Kidney, Bladder	Kidney, Bladder

NOTE: We don't cleanse the heart per say. The spleen is part of the lymphatic system, and is not cleansed in TCM.

BEST SEASON TO CLEANSE

I have had many students say they only have time to do one cleanse each year because of their schedule. They are curious as to what the best time is to do a cleanse. If you can only do one or two cleanses a year, focus on spring or fall. Fall, even more so than spring, is the most critical time because it is a state of dying or decline in nature. This decline is mirrored in our own bodies. The transition from summer to fall is the most difficult for our bodies to handle, especially in northern climates. If one works with the sick, they see how many get worse in the fall and winter months. The fall cleanse is vital for a healthy immune system to fight off the numerous viruses of winter. But the real answer to the question is anytime you fit it into your schedule.

It is ideal to start three days before the actual calendar beginning of each season. For example, if you wanted to do a cleanse in spring, you would start your cleanse three days before the spring equinox (listed as the first day of spring on calanders). Ayurvedic medicine teaches that three to seven days before and after each change of season is when the body is most receptive to detox therapies and Pancha Karma. If possible, it is best to cleanse four to five times each year (including Indian Summer which changes from season to season based on weather) at the change of each season.

Once you have experience with cleansing for a number of years, you can use weather and nature changes as an indicator to start detoxing instead of calendar dates. Traditionally, Native Americans also used nature signs as an indicator for fasting or cleansing. In parts of the world with four seasons, nature gives us two clear signs to start cleansing. Spring cleanses should begin the first day the grass begins to turn vibrant green or once the tulips start blooming from their long winter slumber. Fall cleanses are best to start when the squirrels start burying their nuts in the ground and when the very first leaves start to turn colors.

It has traditionally always been considered wise not to do intense cleanses during the winter months in colder climates. There are various rationale and good reasons for this. However, in my clinical experience with patients and seeing how severely imbalanced most Americans are, I feel we now live in a time where it is more healing to do cleanses in winter than to not do them at all. Most Americans can't afford to miss a season of cleansing.

CHAPTER SEVEN

Who Should Cleanse & Why?

Contrary to popular belief, now is the most important time in human history to cleanse. The body's detox process is one example of how our body achieves it, but our world and our bodies are becoming so toxic, I now feel holistic cleansing is the only way to find balance and regain our divine right to vitality.

In the midst of all our technological growth, we have created a world of pollution and toxins. The world is becoming so polluted that we are at great risk of doing irreversible harm to our Earth. Our bodies are being bombarded by toxins and strange new chemicals at an alarming rate. Despite the efforts of many scientists around the world, major corporations are getting by with polluting our soil, ground water, air, plants, animals and bodies. No human on earth is free of these effects at this time, no matter how remote of an area they live in. On this basic level, cleansing reverses the negative effects of our daily toxin exposure. It also reminds us to be judicious with our selection of the food we eat to fuel our bodies.

Most Americans are becoming so unhealthy that their bodies have no strength to devote to removing these chemicals. Not only are we constantly being overwhelmed by toxins in our environment, we are also living a life of pure excess in the United States. At no other time in our history have we become so inactive and more wasteful. The irony of excess is that it causes deficiency. As technology advances, we use less of our body's healing capabilities. It is no wonder that the US leads the entire world in obesity rates, has the highest rate of stressed citizens, rates high on nationwide depression scales and leads the entire world in rates of chronic diseases. Not to mention for being the most technological and richest country in the world, we don't have the longest life expectancy. We actually rank behind some third world countries.

If cleansing has been popular and proven effective for thousands of years with people eating very clean diets and free from most of contemporary toxins, imagine how important it is in life today. Less than a hundred years ago, most of the world was eating whole foods, the world was relatively toxin free and there was little environmental pollution. The ancients have stressed cleansing programs to remove toxins for over 1,000 years. Just imagine how much we need detox now. In my opinion, cleansing is now a necessary part of human health that should be pursued each season. No preventative health program can be without it.

Anyone who has been exposed to toxins should do a holistic cleanse, and as I discussed earlier, everyone on earth is exposed to toxins. There are a wide variety of illnesses that are either caused by toxins, triggered by toxins or aggravated by toxins. Many diseases can be dramatically healed by a holistic cleanse.

The following are all signs the body is unable to handle toxic exposure. All the following imbalances (both medical and holistic) indicate the possible need for starting a holistic cleanse:

Immune System Weakness
Chronic allergies (both food and environmental)
Weakened immunity
Chronic Fatigue Syndrome
Family history of autoimmune diseases (lupus, rheumatoid arthritis, etc.)
Family history or past history of cancer (any type)
Removal of lymph glands

Eyes
Poor eyesight and some eye problems
Red, irritated eyes

Hair, Skin and Nail Problems
Rashes, dermatitis, eczema, psoriasis, acne
Hair loss and premature balding

Unhealthy or slow-growing fingernails

History of Multiple Prescription Medications
Especially those that affect the liver

Toxin Exposure
Chronic exposure to any type of toxin in the environment
Sensitivity to environmental toxins and sick building syndrome
Excessive medication use
History of illegal drug use
Exposure to plastics manufacturing
Working with heavy metals
Exposure to industrial chemicals
Working with agricultural chemicals such as insecticides and pesticides
Fertilizers and gardening chemicals
Asbestos exposure
Repeated exposure to paints, varnish and glues
Use of chemical solvents such as household cleaning chemicals
Drinking contaminated water

Liver and Gallbladder Dysfunctions
Elevated liver enzymes and/or elevated bilirubin counts
Cirrhosis and/or fatty liver
History of gallstones or gallbladder pains
Hepatitis A, B, C
Frequent alcohol consumption

Aches and Pains
Headaches and migraines
Arthritis, joint and muscle pain
Pains in the upper back and neck
Rib side pain (right and left side both)
Some types of lower back pain

Endocrine Imbalance
Diabetes (both Type I and II)

Thyroid disorders
Adrenal Fatigue Syndrome

Cardiovascular
Ear ringing and high blood pressure
High cholesterol and triglycerides
Arteriosclerosis, poor circulation and heart disease

Other
Fatigue, lowered energy
History of repeated or unnecessary vaccinations (especially hepatitis A)
Present or past smoker
Present consumer of caffeine
Desire to help slow the aging process
Desire to have a healthy baby in the future

How many benefits of cleansing and detox are there? Limitless! For virtually every indication for cleansing covered below, you could use cleansing to help prevent or reverse those particular health conditions. Most every toxin listed throughout this book can be cleansed out of the body and deep tissues. This is just the beginning! Each day new research is showing how cleansing and detox programs can help reverse or treat hundreds of other diseases. The following are common examples:

Creates a sense of emotional balance Although cleansing can cause the release of many suppressed emotions and traumas, almost everyone will feel dramatically more emotionally balanced after a good cleanse. I have seen patients with chronic anxiety, high stress levels, depression and other mood disorders undergo a positive emotional transformation by a simple and appropriate two week cleanse. I saw how cleansing empowered patients to use this new state of happiness to create changes in their lives and spiritual well being. It allows one to shift into new patterns of positive behavior instead of negative downward spirals of destructive habits.

Heals the digestive tract Cleansing can dramatically improve the health, motility and natural rhythms of digestion. You can have a great diet, but you won't assimilate many of those healing nutrients with a weak digestive system. Cleansing, especially with its balanced diet approach, helps constipation, Irritable Bowel Syndrome (IBS), Inflammatory Bowel Disease (IBD), Leaky Gut Syndrome (LGS), acid reflux, indigestion, dysbiosis, malabsorbtion, and a variety of other digestive complaints including poor digestion (especially with fats and oils), gas, bloating, cramping and belching. Signs of an unhealthy diet that suggest a need for cleansing include frequent consumption of non-organic meat products, food additives, food dyes, food coloring, artificial colors, artificial flavors, processed foods, fast foods, microwavable foods, and genetically engineered foods.

Healing skin problems Patients with a variety of skin diseases usually have dramatic improvement after a cleanse. I have seen eczema, psoriasis, acne and dermatitis all dramatically disappear after a cleanse. Since a holistic cleanse causes true healing, these skin conditions often will not come back unless people start eating poorly again. Cleansing will often temporarily cause skin problems to worsen because it causes toxins to be pushed out the skin by the lymphatic system.

Helps prevent certain types of cancer Risks for cancers of the breast, lung, colon, prostate, neck, tongue, head and liver have all been shown to be reduced with many diet changes and specific cleansing supplements discussed in later chapters. Many of the supplements are also used by natural doctors as part of a comprehensive treatment plan for cancer.

Hormone imbalances Herbalists have used liver cleansing herbs to help women with hormone imbalances for hundreds of years. These cleansing herbs can even benefit women weaning off hormone medications or suffering from infertility. Since the liver helps to regulate almost all hormone levels, it is one of the most important organs to support. I have seen hundreds of female patients who have decided to go off synthetic hormones, and many have had great discomfort. Even women who use bio-identical hormones can benefit from liver supporting herbs. They help reduce the cancer risks and other side effects of these hormones. It is also common for menopausal women to have a dramatic reduction of hot flashes while cleansing. Hormonal imbalances that show cause for cleansing include PMS, menstrual irregularities and difficulties, fibroids, breast cysts, ovarian cysts, family history of breast cancer and hormone caused cancer, as well as women who have a difficult time with synthetic hormones or going off hormone therapy.

I am often asked since the liver controls hormones if it is dangerous to use liver detox herbs or go on a cleanse if the patient has hormone problems. My response is always an emphatic, No. That is the genius of cleansing the liver; it assists the body in finding the natural level of hormone balance that is unique to each person. When the liver is healthy, the body can more easily adjust and find individual hormone balance.

Helps protect healthy cells Many of the healing chemicals in the cleansing diet and herbs listed later have amazing disease preventing properties. They have been shown to prevent cell abnormalities, stimulate new healthy cell growth, aid in DNA repair, neutralize dangerous free radicals and prevent genetic damage.

CHAPTER EIGHT

Thirteen Qualities of a Healthy & Holistic Cleanse

The necessary qualities of a complete cleanse, to be truly holistic, must meet thirteen clear criteria. These thirteen qualities are vital for everyone to know before starting any cleanse. You may examine past cleanses you have done and ask if they were truly holistic in nature. These thirteen qualities also allow anyone to identify detox programs that may be harmful or offer little benefit to health. They are a simple checklist for safety and to guarantee your cleanse is complete.

If your cleansing program does not meet all these thirteen traits, then you are not getting the most out of your efforts.

ONE

It has a Clearly Specified Time Length I have seen many patients haphazardly jump into detox programs and would not stop. They thought all the symptoms were good indicators of cleansing. By doing this, they are often weakening their bodies or creating more health problems. I have also seen the opposite. These patients would quit a cleansing program at the first small discomfort.

First time cleansers should not do a cleanse for more than 14 days. Being catabolic, cleansing for too long actually breaks down the body's tissues and makes the body weaker over time. Most cleansing programs are either too short, too long or have no clear stopping point. I once had a patient who had been cleansing for over two years, nonstop. He came to see me because he wasn't feeling well!

As a general rule, there is a safe limit of five cleanses per year. This reflects the time-honored tradition of cleansing once for each of the five seasons. This allows the body sufficient breaks to rebuild and properly rejuvenate. Any more than five cleanses per year will cause the breakdown of healthy body tissues.

You should already be able to see how many of these one or two day detox programs are simply ineffective or unsafe. You can't detoxify anything in a day or two. I call these "fast food cleanses" because they have the same mentality of many junk food restaurants. These short cleanses are based on the underlying mentality of numerous Americans – everything must be instant. All healing or deep cleansing takes time. It takes at least fourteen days to create deep metabolic changes with the body.

TWO

Every Holistic Cleanse Has a Clear Diet Change If you are not changing your diet during a cleanse, then you are not really doing much of anything! The nutrition changes create about 25 – 40% of all the cleansing results. Don't ever think you can take some cleansing pill and still eat fast food, fried food or candy all day long. Great care and thought has to be put into creating a perfect cleansing diet. If it is too restrictive of providing vital nutrients, the body will get weaker. If it incorporates many allergic or poorly digestible foods, then no cleansing will happen. If processed foods are not eliminated, then no detoxifying effect will happen.

THREE

Alterative Herbs are Necessary For Detox Alterative herbs are a special category of herbal medicine that has been used for hundreds of years for detox programs. Remember another of our cleansing sayings: "Without alterative herbs, the deep tissues of the body are never cleansed."

FOUR

Every Holistic Cleanse Has a Short Period of Fasting No holistic cleanse should have more than three days of water or juice fasting. If people are beginners to cleansing diets, they should never fast for more than one day. Experienced cleansers should never fast for more than three days without supervision. Diabetics should not fast at all. My clinical experience has shown that any juice cleansing over seven days in length has few, if any, healing effects. I can't recall how many patients I have seen who thought they would overcome their disease by fasting to "starve the illness into death." This is simply not true. Most people end up only starving their bodies.

Even though some practices may have prolonged fasting, it does not mean they are dangerous. It just means they are not a holistic cleanse program. Many spiritual traditions, especially those of the Native Americans, may require prolonged fasting. I honor their practices and deeply respect them.

FIVE

Every Holistic Cleanse Should Incorporate Home Spa Therapies
If everyone could afford it, it would be ideal to go to a plush cleansing spa for two weeks where your every need could be pampered and all meals could be prepared. Unfortunately, most Americans can't afford an all day spa treatment, much less a two week spa luxury retreat. And neither can I. In reality, most of the expensive spas in America are only for beauty and relaxation, and they don't really stimulate much detox. In fact, many of the "detox" products they use are toxic. There are numourous home Panca Karma spa remedies listed in chapter 15, and each is inexpensive.

SIX

Any Holistic Cleanse Focuses on Gentle Whole Body Detox and the Deep Tissues of the Body When patients come into my office with a grocery bag of supplements, I always ask them why they are taking everything. When they say, "I am cleansing my whole body," I usually get very concerned. This shows me they are not sure what their cleansing program is designed for.

Once people have completed a holistic cleanse program, they can do a more specific detox program if they choose. Someone may choose to do a cleanse that focuses on the liver, kidneys, lymphatic system or colon. It is unwise for people to start out cleansing specific organs because it often causes too rapid of detox. When most people first do a liver cleanse, they often get extremely sick or even have possible side effects.

There are many "five system cleanse" products on the market, but most all are diluted. The biggest problem is that most are not created by herbalists and are frequently created by someone in an office setting. If you examine these supplement labels, they have about 25 or more ingredients. Herbal medicine is an extremely complex topic and combining herbs in formulas takes years of clinical experience. You have to really understand how each herb interacts and affects the body. As a result, most of these cleansing products don't really do much except make you poop or pee frequently.

Any holistic cleanse and detox program must focus on the deep tissues. Remember the cleansing motto, "If it is not detoxifying the deep tissues, then you are not cleansing."

Experienced cleansers may also focus on a certain toxin such as candida, heavy metals, pesticide residues, plastics exposure, specific known liver toxins, industrial chemical poisoning, a specific virus, etc.

SEVEN

Every Holistic Cleanse Must Embrace Introspection, Self Reflection, Emotional Transformation, and Spiritual Healing A cleanse is a catalyst for positive change on all levels or our being – body, mind and spirit. I have seen hundreds of patients undergo dramatic physical and emotional transformations during their cleanse. In fact, this is the area most people are surprised to see such a positive change in. They expect to feel physically better and see their diseases heal, but they are shocked to feel so much more balanced emotionally. Many patients find a complete renewal of their spiritual passion. Emotional balance is our birthright, and you should always expect it from your cleanse.

This is the area that nearly everyone neglects during cleansing. This is one of the most important facets of any holistic program especially if you are trying to create either a catalyst or spark of change in your life. Doing a cleanse without reflecting on your life or spiritual nature is to miss the point. Every culture and religion throughout time has emphasized some type of cleansing or fasting. Most people doing "detox" supplements have no idea of how amazing and transforming a holistic cleanse really is. It is one of the most powerful and positive experiences a person can go through, if it is done right.

A good cleanse is similar to a bear going into his cave to hibernate. It is a time of rest, recovery and regaining our strength for the wonderful opportunities of the new upcoming spring. Like an animal that hibernates, many people find it helpful to withdraw from daily activities as much as they can.

This goal can be achieved by spending more time devoted to prayer, reading spiritually uplifting books, going to a temple/church or starting meditation practices. Many patients find journaling very helpful. Others find it helpful to do daily practice of t'ai chi, yoga or chi kung. You can even sit outside on the patio and watch the squirrels run around all day long. Whatever works for you and is personally revitalizing to your system is acceptable. Later in the book, I will detail many of these invigorating practices.

Cleansing always involves letting go of old thoughts, emotions and "old crap." One has to transform their mind to transform their body. Get excited about letting go of old emotions and thoughts.

EIGHT

Every Holistic Cleanse Has a Slow Transition To Begin a Cleanse and To End a Cleanse The worst thing you can ever do is go from a cleansing diet to eating greasy, processed or fried foods. You will get instant digestive cramps, nausea and liver/gallbladder spasms.

It is just like stretching out and warming up for sports. You would never think of just running a ten mile marathon without training. You would likely quit, pull a muscle, hurt yourself or even collapse. This is why so many people have bad experiences with cleansing. When you see people recommending strange two day purgative cleanses, your warning indicators should go off inside your head. Cleansing can be dangerous if people don't follow a smooth transition onto and off cleansing.

I once had a patient who thought she was ready for a liver cleanse. I knew she wouldn't be able to stay on a cleansing diet 100%, but I could never imagine what she would do. On the last day of her juice fast at the peak of detox, she decided to quit all of a sudden that night. To make things worse, she decided to go eat two McDonald's cheeseburgers and a big order of fries cooked in grease. She called me from the floor of her bathroom on her cell phone. She got instant liver and gallbladder spasms, extreme nausea and was having severe loose stools. I talked to her the next day, and she said she was up for about four hours that night sitting on the toilet.

Don't ever go off a cleansing diet right away. This minimizes the risks for major detox reactions. Simply put, it is the only safe way to do a cleanse of any kind. If you go off a cleanse too quickly, you will often make your liver worse than when you started! This actually creates a potentially dangerous stress on the liver, gallbladder and digestive tract, not to mention your emotions.

Never go on a drinking binge or use illegal drugs during a holistic cleanse. It is one of the worst things you could ever do. You will get extremely sick the next day and have the worst hangover. The only thing worse is to break a juice fast with a greasy fast food cheeseburger, fries and a bunch of beer. You would have to do two cleanses just to reverse the negative effects.

Switch to all natural household cleaners, laundry products, hygiene products, cosmetics and hair care products. Many health food stores have a variety of options and many products can be made from home for very cheap.

NINE

The Strength and Intensity of the Cleanse Must Match the Person's Goals and Past Experience Failure is never good. Most cleanses are so strict, no one can follow them. With each cleanse, a person should gradually try to improve the strictness of their efforts.

One function of this is comfort. This also allows you to experience the full range of detox symptoms and changes each time. As you become more experienced with cleansing reactions, you can be more comfortable with longer and more intense cleanses.

TEN

The Strength and Intensity of the Cleanse Must Match the Person's Current State of Health A person who is weakened by undergoing chemotherapy or radiation treatments for cancer should never start a cleanse until they regain strength. Those with severe fatigue, eating disorders, malnutrition, severe immune diseases, Chronic Fatigue Syndrome, cancer, leukemia, bone marrow disorders and the elderly should take great care before even considering a cleanse. Many of these diseases need a series of tonic formulas to strenghten the body before cleanses can be done.

Later in this book, I have an entire chapter discussing all the medical conditions one should be cautious with before starting a cleanse. If you have these conditions, it doesn't mean you can't do a cleanse. It simply means you need to use more caution, start with lower dosages and/or seek out a natural healthcare provider.

ELEVEN

Every Holistic Cleanse Should Have a List of Personal Goals Again, we are using the cleanse as a catalyst to not only heal our body, but our entire life! You should set a list of a few goals you want to achieve after your cleanse. Some common goals patients have are to relax more, lose weight, feel more energy, have normal bowel movements, reduce the use of toxic cleaning chemicals, eat better after a cleanse, heal a particular skin condition, spend more time in nature, save more money, watch less TV, spend more time with family, spend more time for spiritual practices, love oneself, and so forth. It can be anything that empowers you! The goals can be health goals or personal goals. This is to reinforce the idea that a cleanse, if it is truly holistic, is a way to catalyze positive change in your life.

TWELVE

Every Holistic Cleanse Should Have Specific Lifestyle Changes to Minimize Toxic Exposure There are thousands of toxins in our immediate environment and houses today. If one really wants to cleanse the body, you should not be adding more toxins everyday to your body. There is no better way to stay healthy after your cleanse then to follow a healthy diet and to minimize toxins in your life.

THIRTEEN

Every Holistic Cleanse Includes Nature There is an old saying in natural medicine, "Doctors diagnose and Nature heals." All holistic healing involves nature. In later chapters, I will explain how important it is to actually spend time in nature while cleansing. This can be as simple as going hiking or walking around the lake. Throughout time and in most of Europe today, all detox centers have been located in areas of natural beauty by lakes, warm springs, rivers or mountains. One of the most famous examples is the healing detox spas of Germany in the majestic Black Forest. One is actually over 600 years old! Remember, just being in nature is healing. If you can even spend one day in nature on a picnic during the cleanse, you have succeeded.

CHAPTER NINE

THE FOUR WINDS HOLISTIC CLEANSE

Over several years and the length of my practice, I created a complete, holistic detox program called the Four Winds Holistic Cleanse (FWH Cleanse). It is a unique program from the hundreds of other cleansing programs in the world because it addresses transforming every level of our being. It is a highly specific program that can meet the huge variety of health needs most Americans have. Embracing health, logic and safety, it was developed to maximize quick results, and also prepares one for everything that can happen during a cleanse.

Many people after completing the cleanse feel rejuvenated and full of energy for the first time in their lives. They often have a deeper sense of emotional balance and notice that many of their health complaints have disappeared. I have seen literally hundreds of illnesses improve by simply following the FWH Cleanse for two weeks each season. We scientifically know that every seven years the body replaces and rejuvenates every single cell making us an entirely new person. With the FWH Cleanse, I have seen patients with chronic diseases and those who felt generally awful completely rejuvenate their entire body in as little as three years.

It is safe, effective, inexpensive and can be used during any season and in any climate. It incorporates thousands of years of wisdom and experience from cleansing programs practiced around the world. The famous Scudder's Alterative formula has remained so affective that it is part of the herbal formulas. Many of the seasonal diet changes, lifestyle suggestions and rejuvenation practices are based on the insights of

Traditional Chinese Medicine. And a large part is based on integrating the diverse detox therapies still used in European healthcare today.

The principles of traditional Native American medicine are used here – to have a clear goal to achieve from cleansing, to live in harmony with the seasons of nature, to regain health, to make strict dietary changes, to embrace herbs as agents of divine healing and to foster rapid spiritual growth.

I incorporated many of the practices, insights and herbal formulas that work well for Americans from Pancha Karma. There are few Pancha Karma centers in the United States, and at prices of upards of $1000 per day, this therapy is not accessible to most Americans. I suggest it to anyone who can afford it, but the FWH Cleanse utilizes many of the same practices and all can be done from home. Better yet, they each cost pennies. These home spa therapies can range from massage to herbal steam baths to dry skin brushing. All help us feel better on the cleanse, but most importantly they stimulate a deeper detox. They are easy to incorporate after the cleanse and help minimize toxic accumulation.

I created this program so that it was gentle. It is designed to minimize health risks by supporting all the body's detox processes. It was developed to be safe so many with chronic or serious diseases can follow it. With that in mind, I created the FWH Cleanse so any person could safely follow it without supervision or worry. I deally, if I was working with a patient, I would custom make an herbal cleansing formula just for them. But the FWH Cleanse was created with a specific combination of herbal supplements that combine perfectly to achieve this effect and work for everyone.

In my clinical experience, most patients lose three to seven pounds on a two week beginners cleanse. Some have lost up to 20 pounds during an advanced three week cleanse. Most women will have a drastic reduction of hot flashes and hormone symptoms. It quickly supports the body to return to a state of hormone balance by assisting the liver in the metabolism of many hormones.

The FWH Cleanse focuses on supporting the whole body and targeting a wide variety of all known toxins. Most detox programs do not help detoxify the deep tissues, but the FWH Cleanse does.

This FWH Cleanse diet addresses all of the important factors to create the perfect detox eating program that can be followed for two weeks or longer with no risk of nutritional deficiency. As we will discuss later, even though the diet looks mild compared to other detox programs, it can still be hard to follow. The emphasis is on slowly going off the regular diet, onto a cleansing diet and slowly back onto a regular diet. This program is specifically designed to allow the body to warm up, reach an intense cleansing phase and then cool back down before going onto regular food again.

The herbal supplement dosages are also designed to slowly "warm up" the body into a state of gradual detox, reach an apex of more intensive cleansing and then slowly "cool down" as you go off the products.

There are many options advanced cleansers can add to make the detox stronger. You should never try adding the advanced cleansing methods until you have successfully finished a beginners cleanse. That is why I designed it both for beginners and with added options for those who successfully complete it. If a person wants a deeper cleanse, they can simply incorporate more of the lifestyle changes I mention in later chapters. You can do more saunas, steam baths, increase the dosage of detox supplements, etc. Maybe you decide to remove all toxic cleaning products from your home, use only all natural shampoo and buy local organic food. For most people, it simply means following the diet more strictly. The program itself is designed so beginners can easily follow it, but those with years of experience will still be challenged to take their body to deeper levels of detox.

The "working smarter, not harder" mindset is what this cleanse was built on. Those with more serious diseases or on numerous medications may want to consult with a natural healthcare provider who has experience in working with patients on detox programs. Tell them you want to follow this program, but you would like their guidance. This can often be a great source of security since cleansing symptoms can cause a scare. Also for those really motivated cleansers, you may consult with a natural healthcare provider to have them make customized cleansing products and supplements.

CHAPTER TEN

WHAT TO EXPECT DURING THE CLEANSE

In holistic cleansing, healing is often compared to peeling an onion. As we peel though the layers of our illnesses, we often discover deep or older issues. This is very similar to counseling. You may go to see a counselor for panic attacks. After you learn to relax and develop skills to keep anxiety at bay, you may discover these feelings come from some deep past trauma.

Holistic cleansing is similar. Patients are amazed, bewildered and sometimes even frightened when they begin to experience symptoms of an illness from years before. As our bodies start to release toxins stored deep in our tissues, emotions and symptoms of past illnesses may resurface. In natural healing, this is called, "Working out the old illness." Most illnesses are never really completely cured. Most people usually take a medication that suppresses the symptoms and so most Americans continue to add new layers of illness over these old imbalances. You can imagine how many layers of imbalances people have by the time they are in middle age.

When the body undergoes a healthy holistic cleanse process, it will release all the memory and imbalance of the disease. It is a unique aspect of natural healing that western medicine does not quite yet understand. We have to go deep into our bodies to remove these old patterns so that new tissues and healing can begin.

One elderly gentleman who suffered from polio as a child had never really regained his health when I met him a few years ago. In the second week of the Four Winds Holistic Cleanse, he began experiencing an array of symptoms that reminded him of his suffering from polio. As is usual with detox, his symptoms were much less severe then in the past. His body was cleansing away the old diseased tissues and releasing the immune system pattern of that illness. After about five days, everything returned to normal. When the cleanse was over, he felt a renewed sense of vitality he had not felt since the age of 16. The memories also created a great deal of emotional release which greatly helped his chronic depression.

Another patient suffered from severe pleurisy as a child. He began experiencing the same pleurisy-like symptoms during his first cleanse. We had discussed the "peeling the onion" effect before he started so he was prepared. Interestingly, he also released a great deal of childhood fears he carried around all his life ever since his struggles.

I'm sure that no one wants to experience past disease symptoms, but fear not. This flaring up of old disease symptoms is just the disease leaving the body. It is the body's way of communicating that this pattern is gone or the layer of illness is released. Pete Medicine Eagle, the medicine man I studied with, has often said that, "It is the last attempt of the disease to fight for its life." It is really a wonderful blessing because it represents the disease truly leaving all traces of itself from the body. These symptoms will usually only last for one to three days. If these changes overwhelm you, you can quit cleansing for a day and everything will return to normal.

CLEANSING SYMPTOMS

Good cleansing programs create noticeable changes in the body. This is the goal of any detox program. However, when you don't expect to have detox symptoms, it can cause a scare.

The following is a list of all the possible symptoms that can occur during the cleanse. Remember, most people will experience only three to five of these symptoms at once. The more toxic you are, the stronger the detox reactions you will likely have. The intensity of these changes is usually not extreme or overwhelming. Some are exciting. Don't let it scare you away from starting the cleansing program. Remember what one of my teachers told me: "Trust the Process." In fact, it is a positive indicator to have detox symptoms during your cleansing program. They indicate your body and organs are trying to change and that the toxins are leaving your body. Such detox symptoms can range from a variety of responses from physical, emotional or even spiritual changes.

COMPREHENSIVE LIST OF CLEANSING SYMPTOMS

System	Detox Symptom
General	Slight fatigue, mild temporary feelings of disorientation, feeling very tired or sleepy at night
Skin	Acne, boils, cysts, worsening of psoriasis, worsening of eczema, appearance of red pimples, bumps and small scalp sores
Muscle & Joint	Muscle aches, joint tenderness, mild joint aches
Breast	Tenderness, cysts, growths
Pancreas	Slight drops in blood sugar causing mild dizziness
Lymphatic System	Swollen and tender lymph nodes, swollen lymphatic vessels
Head	Migraines, headaches (especially on sides and front of head)
Ears	Slight temporary buzzing in ears, small pimples on ears, itching inside the ears
Eyes	Redness, irritation, allergy like symptoms, occasional twinges/spasms
Nervous System	Mild anxiety, sometimes depression, old emotions or past experience may be brought up to one's conscious, temporary giddiness (like when people have spring cleaning fever), rare euphoria
Emotions	Emotional processing, anger, frustration, irritation or any other release is possible
Mouth & Lips	Small sores, bad breath, canker sores

Liver & Gallbladder	Mild liver area cramps and spasms which feel like "little pulsations" or as one patient said "a cell phone vibrating in my liver"
Stomach	Slight nausea, mild feelings of fullness, bloating, gas, burping
Kidneys & Bladder	Increased urination, rare slight retention of water, slight soreness in lower back, darker urine, thicker urine, stinky or highly aromatic urine
Intestines	Diarrhea, loose stools, slight digestive cramps, odd bowel movements, very large bowel movements
Heart & Circulatory System	Rare mild drop in blood pressure
Immune System	Flu like sensations with muscle aches, sweating and chills (this is very common in those with past viral infection), alternating hot and cold sensations
Hormones	Menstrual changes and cycle changes, mild ovarian or uterine spasms, temporary loss of sex drive, spontaneous menstrual cycle
Spiritual	Increased sense of spiritual devotion and clarity

I can here everyone now say, "Sounds like I will have to quit work!" I want to reassure you that these symptoms are usually very mild. All cleansing symptoms are temporary, and they often go away in a day or two. Even though people may notice a few of these minor detox symptoms, many will still experience an overall sense of vitality.

Not all cleansing symptoms are uncomfortable. The following is a short list of cleansing symptoms patients are usually happy to see:

Increase in energy, sense of euphoria, weight loss, improved digestion, bowel regularity, mental clarity, stress reduction, increase in libido, improved immune function, less allergy symptoms, less environmental and food allergy symptoms, spiritual devotion and spontaneous healing of illnesses.

How can some people feel an increase in energy while others feel fatigue? Each person will experience a unique combination of cleansing symptoms based on their current state of health and medical history. Experiences may also vary based on your previous cleansing experience and the number of toxin residues in your body.

THOSE UNDER MEDICAL CARE

For those under medical care, you may need to educate your doctor about temporary changes in your blood tests during your cleanse. The first week, cholesterol levels will be slightly elevated. Liver enzymes may have a very slight increase the first week. After the cleanse, even if you had chronic elevated liver enzymes, they should be much lower or within normal range. This is clear evidence of the liver regenerating effects of cleansing.

For those with a history of viral infections, there will usually be some cold and flu like symptoms. In the medical world, this is called the Herksheimer reaction. It is caused when viruses die and release toxins. People with chronic viral infections, herpes, genital herpes, hepatitis, Human Papilloma Virus (HPV), AIDS/HIV or other viral infections will likely experience the Herksheimer reaction. Patients will complain of feeling warmth, flushing, mild sweating, body aches, alternating chills, sore muscles and other symptoms. Like all cleansing symptoms, they are temporary. If you go off the detox formulas for a day, you will feel fine. Patients who have this stronger Herksheimer reaction usually feel great after the cleanse.

TEN MOST COMMON DETOX SYMPTOMS

"Will I get all these things?" you might ask. Based on my work with patients, I have found there are ten common detox symptoms most patients get, and there will usually be between three and five of each symptoms per cleanse.

Most Common Cleansing Experience

1. Skin rashes, blemishes, small irritations and acne
2. More frequent bowel movements with much greater volume and changes in texture
3. Emotional releases
4. Small liver "twinges"
5. Headaches
6. Muscle aches and soreness
7. Mild flu like symptoms
8. "Spring fever" with tons of excess energy that is almost anxiety like
9. Urinary changes and mild lower back ache
10. Fatigue

THE HEALING CRISIS

The Healing Crisis is a temporary, more powerful combination of three or more cleansing symptoms at once. It is caused when the body, all of a sudden, releases a large amount of stored toxins, stagnant accumulations deep in the tissues and emotions. A healing crisis will usually only last for one or two days. Imagine your body as a river dam. Sometimes small amounts of toxins are continually released through. At other times, it can be as though the dam breaks and everything floods out. This temporary "wave" is a large amount of toxins leaving at once. The body has chosen to go into detox overdrive and influence the metabolism of many types of toxins. The healing crisis is like a storm moving through the body. If you can just hold on long enough, you will be fine and the sun will again be shining. A healing crisis will usually happen in those who have had a high exposure to more dangerous toxins or had chronic exposure to a variety of toxins. People with a history of cancer or liver diseases will usually have a healing crisis.

It is common for almost everyone to experience the healing crisis during one of their first three cleanses. Remember that it is a good sign and only temporary. It is called a "crisis" because it can at times be intense and uncomfortable. I personally prefer it to be referred as a "healing burst" because it is a positive change. When patients are having detox symptoms, they usually say that they had a few cleansing changes. And when patients have a healing crisis, they remark with surprise that it was a huge transformation.

What to Do During a Healing Crisis

If the healing crisis becomes overwhelming, simply stop taking the cleansing herbal formulas for a day. This will stop the healing crisis in 99% of all incidences. Stop only the supplements, but do not stop the cleansing diet or other accessory treatments. The day after stopping, add back the herbal cleansing formulas at half the recommended dosage. One of the key indicators of the healing crisis is that all the symptoms will leave just as quickly as they came. Remember that the healing crisis is a positive change.

Healing a Crisis Patient

A fifty-five year old woman came to see me to start a cleansing program. She had no cleansing experience except for taking a few supplements from a health food store. We used a slightly modified form of the FWH Cleanse. After day five, she called the clinic and asked what was going on. Her liver was vibrating, she had a headache, felt flu like, had acne like she did when she was twelve and was having bowel movements three times a day. Her menopausal hot flashes were somehow gone. She had a huge emotional release about some childhood issues with her father. She asked if this was cleansing and what she should do. I assured her everything was right on track. I reminded her she could quit taking the cleansing supplements for a day if everything was too intense. She came back to the clinic the next week after the cleanse was over. She was excited. She lost seven pounds, her hot flashes had not returned, her lifelong constipation seemed gone, her energy level was much higher and she felt emotionally balanced for the first time. She was excited about her next cleanse.

This is just one example. Sometimes symptoms are more intense. Not everyone will have a healing crisis every time they cleanse. Usually, people have less detox symptoms each time because their bodies are becoming healthier.

CHAPTER ELEVEN

Cleansing As Catalyst to Personal Growth & Healing

The Four Winds Holistic Cleanse acts as a catalyst for positive changes in all areas of one's life. Unfortunately, this is an area that most people overlook when cleansing. Cleansing is often a very dramatic life altering process, whether it is healing a disease or transforming old emotional scars. Our organs and deep tissues hold many emotions and past traumas. There is an old and wise saying in natural healing, "Your issues become your tissues." We cannot truly heal our bodies unless we release old traumas and pains.

Positive Affirmations and Emotional Growth

There is no cleansing, transformation or healing that can take place without changing the way we think. Negative attitudes, chronic internalized stress, excess emotions and self-defeating thoughts create a strong field of energy around us and within our beings. A bad attitude can affect our health just as much as some toxins. In a holistic sense, this is why these attitudes and thoughts are also considered toxins. We can do cleanses forever, but if we still think negatively we will often be stuck in that same disease pattern. Emotions, thoughts and beliefs must be transformed, explored and released. Otherwise, they will further perpetuate self-destructive behaviors and poor lifestyle choices after the cleanse.

This often overlooked part of the natural healing process can cause great suffering in hundreds of patients. In fact, during the healing process, the subconscious part of our mind really puts up a fight. Positive thinking and daily affirmations help to keep these self-destructive thoughts in check. I have seen patients who had been on extremely restrictive diets for many years. They took supplements daily, they didn't drink, they didn't take drugs, they ate a very strict diet, they spent time relaxing and they had tremendously faithful workout regimens. Yet, many of these people were still sick everyday or suffering from the same health complaints. Whether people were on restrictive candida diets or overly extreme fasting routines, they still suffered. Thanks to many of my teachers, I was able to spot instantly how their negative self-beliefs and negative thinking were constantly reinforcing the destructive side of their subconscious. Negative thinking reinforces and gives power to disease.

In Traditional Chinese Medicine and Ayurveda, there has been a long understanding of how specific emotions and negative thoughts can affect the internal organs. Emotions, by affecting our internal organs, slowly begin to cause diseases in ways we are just beginning to understand in the western world. In Ayurveda, we understand this dynamic by examining the effects of emotions on the chakras and the doshas. The charkras are "switching boards" of the nervous system where stress and emotions first affect our health. The doshas are the three fundamental forces of our body, commonly known as Kapha, Vata and Pitta. Health is the balance of the three.

In TCM, we understand how specific emotions contribute to the health or disease process of specific organs.

EFFECTS OF SPECIFIC EMOTIONS ON HEALTH IN TCM

Organ	Emotion that Damages
Liver & Gallbladder	Anger, frustration, resentment, lack of courage, overly critical
Kidney & Bladder	Fear, excessive worry, panic
Lung & Large Intestine	Grief, sadness, sorrow, attachment, excessive nostalgia for the past
Heart, Pericardium & Small Intestine	Excessive joy, manic states, paranoia, anxiety

Spleen, Stomach & Pancreas	Worry, excessive thinking, excessive mental activity, lack of being nourished

It is indeed truly amazing that researchers and doctors simply label many illnesses as having "psychosomatic" or "stress" -related causes. For over two thousand years in TCM, there has been an understanding for how these emotions can trigger health and disease. By addressing the mind and thoughts, we can finally create a true holistic and transformative healing process.

TRANSFORMING EMOTIONS THROUGH CLEANSING

By studying TCM, we see it is a "vis a vis" system. This means the physical health of an organ affects the specific emotions of each organ. Likewise, the certain emotions of each organ will affect the organ's physical health. For example, if you are angry all the time, your liver will be more likely to develop a disease. The exciting idea is by detoxifying each organ during the cleanse, we begin to positively change all the emotions of that organ. So by cleansing the liver, we begin to release all that stored anger and frustration. Since the FWH Cleanse detoxifies all internal organs, we can begin to transform all emotions and stress. This reason alone is why cleansing is so vital in today's stressed world. We are creating a new physical body and emotional body through cleansing.

What does all this mean to the rookie or veteran cleanser? It simply means you need to embrace positive thinking and relaxation as well as use positive visualization and set goals for healing. I always encourage patients to make a list of goals they want to achieve in their life. They can be personal, related to health and lifestyle or anything you can imagine. Write them on paper the night before you start the cleanse. Review them at least once per day during your cleanse to keep your subconscious mind focused on healing and to keep you motivated.

I have developed a favorite affirmation I encourage patients to say during their cleanse. Some people like to say it after prayer or meditation. Some find it empowering to say it each time before they take their detox supplements, before they eat or first thing in the morning. These affirmations create a powerful vibration that taps into the latent healing powers of our subconscious. Remember that we only use about 5-10% of our brain on a daily basis.

> ### THE FOUR WINDS HOLISTIC CLEANSE POSITIVE AFFIRMATION
>
> *I am cleansing my liver, gallbladder, blood, kidneys, deep tissues, small intestine, large intestine, lymphatic system and entire body of all toxins. My body's intelligence is releasing all stored toxins, negative thoughts, emotions and past traumas. I am rejuvenating every cell of my body so I can reach my fullest potential. All that does not serve my health, I choose to release during this cleanse. I am achieving all my personal and health goals.*

You may choose to write your own healing affirmation. This particular affirmation is simply one many patients have found to be helpful. It is best to write out your positive affirmation and post it on your wall or work desk. This allows you to see it all day long.

HEALING VISUALIZATION

I have observed many patients heal faster through daily positive visualization with their affirmation. There are countless ways to do this. The only important element is that it feels right to you. Some people like to start at their head and see a healing light go through their entire body. As the light moves down, it heals all the internal organs. Every cell of the body and every organ becomes illuminated in radiant light. This healing light moves all the way to the bottom of the feet. It is important to see every organ and tissue smile at you. Bring compassion and love to each organ of your body. Other patients have benefited from doing daily prayer, using relaxation tapes or even visualizing angels healing their body.

THE MOST DANGEROUS PART OF CLEANSING – DIRTY SELF-THOUGHTS

Later we will discuss a few precautions those with certain disease conditions should be aware of before starting. The most dangerous part of cleansing is when people begin to see themselves as dirty, unclean, guilty or shameful. We all feel internally dirty to some degree because it is our bodies' way of intuitively communicating there is toxic garbage building in our systems. However, I have seen patients who became addicted to cleansing, restrictive diets and laxatives because they feel "dirty" inside.

This tendency is more common in those with the following history: psychological illness, eating disorders, unbalanced religious beliefs, cult worship, improper family beliefs, victims of sexual abuse, addictive personalities, obsessive compulsive disorders as well as abuse by family members and others. These people often go through life unhappy, feeling impure, dirty and sinful. These are the people who often take cleansing overboard and develop addictive habits towards it. They are constantly taking their bodies to unnatural extremes in an effort to try and remove this part of their being. After each cleanse, they end up feeling those same unclean emotions and keep going at it again. This is a psychological imbalance that needs to be recognized.

I do not discuss this as a judgment. It is a behavior I have observed in some patients. I have also seen many healthcare practitioners push their own negative past onto patients causing them to think they are impure and need cleansing to remove these evils. If someone starts talking like that, get up and run out of their office immediately. It is important for both patients and practitioners to be aware of this so that if they see this pattern in themselves or patients, they can address it immediately.

If you personally know you fall into this category, you can still safely do a cleanse. However, you should also see a counselor to address these issues while you are cleansing. I ask everyone to remember that everything affects our health, so we must also heal our thoughts and emotions. It is exciting to know the FWH Cleanse is devised with both safety and effectiveness in mind. The entire program is developed to prevent many of these addictive habits from developing. It is also one of the reasons why the cleanse is exactly two weeks long.

CHAPTER TWELVE

CLEANSING SAFETY

CLEANSING REMINDER
All supplements should always be taken at least an hour away from any prescription medications.

SAFETY POINTS

There is a myth that every disease can be "cleansed away." This is not always true. There are a few diseases that can actually get worse by starting a cleanse at the wrong time or for too long. The Four Winds Holistic Cleanse is developed to protect and safeguard everyone from any possible negative effects. The supplements in the cleansing program were also chosen because they have very few interactions with any medications. However, there are a few medical conditions that you should be extra cautious with or consult with a natural healthcare provider before starting a cleanse.

CONTRAINDICATIONS AND CONCERNS BEFORE STARTING THE CLEANSE

People who are extremely toxic, hypersensitive to herbs or on multiple strong medications should be cautious before starting the cleanse. If you are sensitive to medications, supplements or herbs, you should start the cleansing formulas at half the lowest recommended dose. Liver detox can also cause your body to metabolize medications faster because it is better able to break down prescription drugs and their chemical metabolites. The increased fiber in the diet and increased bowel movements can also reduce the absorption of some medications.

People with severe gallbladder obstructions and advanced liver disease should consult with a practitioner before starting a cleanse. Do not start a cleanse if you have an active infection like a cold or flu. Cleansing can make the body a little weaker at first and may prolong the infection. Simply recover from the flu or cold fully before starting the holistic cleanse.

If you are currently undergoing chemotherapy or radiation, do not start the FWH Cleanse until after treatment is over. If you have a long-term cancer that requires a single dose of chemotherapy every three or more weeks, it is advisable to start the holistic cleanse. However, you should consult with a natural healthcare provider first. Never start a cleanse if you are undergoing chemotherapy and have any of these recent symptoms: nausea, diarrhea, malnutrition, malabsorbtion, fatigue, low white blood cell counts, low red blood cell counts, weight loss or anemia. Anyone can safely follow the FWH Cleanse Diet during chemotherapy or radiation treatments to support the body, but you will need to add some extra protein and essential fatty acids.

People with Crohn's disease, diverticulosis, chronic diarrhea or colitis should be careful about making drastic changes to their diet. You may also have to start with half the recommended dosage of fiber supplement for a few days. Slowly begin to add more of the fiber supplement back to full dosage.

People who are bulimic, anorexic or severely underweight should use caution before starting a cleanse. If you have had a recent serious exposure to toxic chemicals, pesticides or any heavy metal poisoning, start your cleansing supplements at half the recommended dosage. You will likely have powerful detox changes due to recent toxin exposure.

Women who are pregnant or nursing should never do a cleanse. Detox therapies can be utilized before conception. Toxins are released during cleansing, circulate through the blood and can be passed on to the developing fetus. During pregnancy, the focus is to nourish by following a whole foods and organic diet.

WORKING WITH YOUR HEALTH CARE PROVIDER

For those of you who have any of these serious health concerns, you can consult with a natural healthcare practitioner who is familiar with cleansing therapies. Just because you have a certain disease or are on multiple medications, it should not prevent you from starting a cleanse! Bring in this book to show your healthcare provider the program you need to follow. They may have some additional insights based on your health history. It is best to work with someone who has their own herbal pharmacy so they can custom compound anything you need. See the resource section at the end of the book for locating a practitioner in your area.

CHAPTER THIRTEEN

THE FOUR WINDS HOLISTIC CLEANSE DIET

"The best of all medicines are rest and fasting."
BENJAMIN FRANKLIN

The Four Winds Holistic Cleanse has its own specific detoxifying diet. The cleansing diet is a basic, all natural, whole foods organic diet. It focuses on foods that support detox and are full of disease fighting phytochemicals. The FWH Cleanse Diet incorporates the wisdom of many ancient traditions, modern clinical practices and the latest in new research. The following list clearly shows all the acceptable foods while cleansing and all those that should be avoided. The diet creates about 35-50% of the detox effects, and it must be followed as closely as possible. Even though it may seem easy for those eating healthily, there are always a few of the dietary changes that are psychologically challenging for everyone! Remember, the diet is only for two weeks.

Since you will be following a whole foods diet, it will require more time cooking at home and preparing meals. Many patients have shared how the diet wonderfully creates an awareness of how many processed and toxic foods they were eating on a daily basis. Incorporating these diet changes after the cleanse can also dramatically reduce your toxin exposure. Many of the healing foods (and supplements in the next chapter) have been shown to reduce certain types of cancer.

GENERAL LIFESTYLE RECOMMENDATIONS

- No smoking or tobacco products.

- Avoid all alcohol and illegal drugs.

- Avoid all coffee, caffeine and decaf coffee.

- All food must be eaten in its whole, pure, unadulterated natural state. Avoid all processed foods.

  o No foods that are instant, microwaveable, prepackaged, fast, fried or canned. Try to avoid all frozen foods if possible.

  o All food should be bought fresh from the store or market.

GENERAL DIETARY RECOMMENDATIONS — FOODS TO AVOID

- Avoid all saturated fats, oils, and heavy meals.

- No candy, chocolate or refined sugar.

- No breads or pastas of any kind, not even sprouted grain breads.

- No carbonated beverages of any kind including colas or diet colas.

- Avoid all acidic foods such as tomatoes, oranges and grapefruits.

- Avoid all diary products including cheese, butter, milk or yogurt.

  o Ghee (also called clarified butter) is acceptable. Small amounts of goat milk are acceptable in cooking.

  o Not even organic dairy products are acceptable.

GENERAL DIETARY RECOMMENDATIONS — FOODS TO EMPHASIZE

- Emphasize eating all vegetables only lightly steamed or lightly cooked. In warmer climates and in summer, one can utilize lots of raw vegetables.

- Emphasize high fiber foods and increased water intake.

- Small amounts of lemon juice are helpful to take before meals.

- Emphasize eating all fresh foods in their whole, natural state.

- Emphasize organically grown food especially meat products. You are trying to shift all the body's reserves into detoxification pathways. If you are eating loads of pesticides and chemicals in your food, your liver will have to expend a lot of energy metabolizing those toxins.

- Emphasize local foods in season, and support local farmers. Microbiologists now have research showing how locally grown foods contain the proper combination of good bacteria from the soil that we need to fight off diseases. Organic is important, but locally grown organic is the best!

- Try to drink only spring, distilled or triple osmosis water. I was shocked to find out how many contaminants were in our house's water when my wife and I had a water test. I was also surprised to find out that even though a city can guarantee relatively clean drinking water, it only applies to testing at the plant and not on its journey to your house. If you have old pipes, they may be leaking lots of metals into your water.

WHY IS THIS THE CLEANSING DIET?

The FWH Cleanse Diet is an amazing combination of many natural healing traditions including naturopathy, clinical herbalism, Native American seasonal diets, the whole foods movement, TCM, Ayurvedic, clinical nutrition protocols, medical nutrition therapy and clinical European medical detox programs. The diet also incorporates the latest research on phytochemicals and natural biological compounds that induce various metabolic and liver detoxification pathways. It is an amazing cornucopia of disease fighting chemicals. The diet is also devised to reduce most common causes of undetected food allergens in the American diet. Most importantly, it is based on my many years of clinical practice designing whole body cleansing programs for patients.

> GOLDEN CLEANSING RULES
> If it doesn't look exactly like it does in nature, don't eat it! If you can't pronounce the ingredient list, you can't have it. If it is not on the list, you can't eat it.

THE FWH CLEANSE DIET

The following is a complete list of all the acceptable foods on the cleansing diet. It is a shopping list of everything you can eat. If it is not on the list, you can't eat it.

Liver Detoxification Foods Asparagus, turnips, carrots, celery, lemons, limes, artichokes and artichoke hearts, parsnips, bamboo shoots, burdock root, yams, adzuki beans, rhubarb, mung beans, beets, lecithin, shitake mushrooms

> *If you are consuming lots of beets you may experience reddish urine (more common in women) and reddish colored stools. These are the red chemical compounds in the beets and not blood.*

Liver Healing/Restoring Foods Beets, chicory root, rhubarb, lyci berry
Cruciferous Vegetables Broccoli, brussel sprouts, cabbage, cauliflower, radish, rutabaga
Beans All beans are acceptable, especially mung and adzuki
Whole Grains Barley, basmati rice, long grain brown rice, amaranth, quinoa, short grain brown rice, millet, wild rice
> *No instant cereals, quick cooking grains or cereals. Only grains in their whole, unprocessed state can be used.*

Fermented Foods Miso, pickled ginger, sauerkraut, kim-chi, pickled beets, raw apple cider vinegar
Sulforaphane Foods Red cabbage, white cabbage, napa cabbage, bok choy, garlic, onions, shallots, ramps, nasturtium, horseradish, chives
Vegetables All vegetables are acceptable. Focus on chicory root,

radish, okra, Jerusalem artichoke root, artichoke, celery, beets, burdock root, broccoli, cauliflower, red cabbage, carrots, yams, sweet potatoes, etc.

> *Try incorporating more root vegetables into your diet. They are also very filling and nourishing while cleansing.*
> *No white potatoes are allowed during the cleanse.*

Fruits Apples, cherries, blackberry, pears, lemons, limes, blueberries, peaches, plumbs, raspberry, gooseberry, watermelon, cantaloupe, muskmelon, pomegranates and boysenberry. No other fruits are allowed.

> *No dried or processed fruits. Only fruits in their whole, raw state.*
> *Any native seasonal fruits are acceptable depending on the part of the U.S. you live in. Absolutely no tomatoes, oranges or grapefruits. They are highly acidic and cause strain on the liver and are also common food allergies.*

Juices Carrot, beet, spinach, celery, vegetable blends, any of the vegetables and fruits listed above.

Again, no tomato, orange or grapefruit juices.

Sprouts All spouts are acceptable, especially bean, sunflower, alfalfa, cabbage and broccoli.

> *Sprouts are some of the most detoxifying foods we have. They can be easily and cheaply grown from your home. You can buy sprout-growing kits at your health food store.*

Fiber Flax seeds, oat bran, apple pectin, grapefruit pectin, rice bran

> *Some people may be sensitive to oat bran or flax seeds. Try a little before adding too much. Always drink your fiber with lots of water.*

Cooking Oils Sesame, flax, walnut, olive, coconut, pumpkin, ghee

These oils can be used for cooking, sautéing, for salad dressings or baking. Never heat flax oil and only use it in salad dressings.

Protein Nuts and seeds (walnut, pecans, pumpkin seeds, almonds, sunflower seeds, pine nuts), all beans, tempeh (a fermented soy product), high quality vegetable proteins, only small amounts of organic tofu, fish (the only acceptable animal protein, emphasize walleye, salmon, cod, halibut, trout, pollock, and other local fish native to your area)

No shellfish (lobster, shrimp, crayfish, crab, etc.) is allowed. Fish should be fresh and should be wild caught. No farm raised fish. Fish should be broiled, lightly grilled or poached only.
Eating sushi and sashimi is great while cleansing. Sushi restaurants are one of the easiest restaurants to eat at while cleansing.
Fresh Alaska fish are the best quality. Pacific caught halibut and cod are better than Atlantic caught.
Nuts and seeds are a great source of protein while cleansing.

Wild Greens/Bitter Greens Arugula, amaranth (pigweed), beet greens, bok choy, mustard greens, dandelion greens, collard, garlic mustard, kale, chickweed, lamb's quarters, turnip greens, endive, mallow, nettles, bitter lettuce greens, parsley, purslane, radicchio, sorrel, spinach, swiss chard, watercress, violet leaf, violet flower, miner's lettuce, wild lettuce, wild grape leaf, yellow dock leaf, or any other wild greens

Eat lots of steamed greens while on the cleanse.

Spices Turmeric, cilantro leaf, coriander, curry, saffron, rosemary, basil, thyme, oregano, garlic, onion, parsley, sage and ginger are the best for detox

Almost any spice is acceptable during the cleanse. The ones listed have more research to support their use for detox. Spices are some of the most detoxifying foods we have. Try to incorporate more spice to take the place of less salt and sugar in your diet. Sea salt may also be used.

Natural Sweeteners Small amounts of stevia, pure maple syrup, small amounts of local honey and barley malt syrup can be used as natural sweeteners

Natural Sauces Braggs brand Liquid Aminos (natural soy sauce), gomasio (sesame seed paste), small amounts of tamari sauce (natural soy sauce)

Tip The Organic Sunshine Burgers brand Garden Herb patty (made from vegetables and sunflower seeds) is the only frozen, prepared food that is cleansing approved. It can be purchased at most health food stores.

Cooking Methods and Tips

Lightly steaming is preferred for all vegetables. Minimal amounts of broiling, light sautéing (only with approved oils), boiling, pressure-cooking and light grilling are also allowed. Try to use bamboo cookware and utensils such as a bamboo vegetable steamer. Never use designer non-stick cooking pans or aluminum cookware. Focus on only stainless steel, copper or cast iron cookware. Most non-stick cookware is highly toxic.

More Notes About Diet

Juices can be consumed with any meal or as a meal themselves. You don't have to wait until your juice fast to start adding juices. Fruits or fruit juices should only be consumed between meals to ensure proper digestion. Small amounts of blueberry or apple may be added to your cleansing juice blends.

If you have never consumed beet juice or other vegetable juices, start by first adding three ounces at a single serving. I have seen patients try to drink 16 ounces of fresh beet juice on their first day and go into immediate detox mode with liver/gallbladder spasms. Begin slowly introducing increasing amounts of juices each day. Some people may become slightly nauseous from the detox effects of juices. Some can only consume small amounts of vegetable juice with meals because of their blood sugar sensitivities. You should not add juices at all if you are a diabetic or hypoglycemic. Instead, eat whole fruits and vegetables.

Many nutrients can also support normal liver detoxification by affecting Phase I and II enzymes. These nutrients include vitamins (B6, folic acid, B12, C), minerals (zinc, magnesium, selenium), lipotropics (choline) and amino acids (glutathione, glycine, methionine, cysteine, taurine). The diet is developed to be naturally high in these critical nutrients so you don't have to buy them as supplements.

OTHER DIETARY NOTES

One of the major goals of any cleanse is reflection. You will notice how difficult the cleansing diet is to follow. The diet brings attention to how poorly we really eat. I consider myself a very healthy eater, yet I am amazed at how difficult it is to find food while cleansing. Eating out is very difficult, if not impossible, depending on where you live. You have to buy almost all your food fresh and cook it yourself. Over the years I have found a small number of restaurants you can find some cleansing friendly foods at.

CLEANSING FRIENDLY RESTAURANTS

Type of Resturant	Cleanse Safe Foods
African	Bean dishes, whole grain dishes
Japanese	Most all sushi and sashimi, fresh fish dishes, miso soup
East Indian	Bean dishes, large variety of healthy vegetarian bean and grain dishes
Thai	Tofu with vegetables, vegetable and basil dishes, coconut soup
Southwest	Bean and vegetable soups
American	Salads

Four Winds Holistic Cleanse Juice Recipe

This is my famous detox juice recipe. If you have a juicer, you can make it at home. Many juice stores and health food stores can also make it for you.

Recipe

- Two medium beets, well washed, using both the beet itself and the green tops
- One small handful of fresh watercress
- Three average sized organic carrots
- One large piece of fresh organic celery
- Two small pieces of fresh ginger about the size of a quarter and sliced very thin
- One large handful of fresh organic spinach, well washed
- One half of a fresh organic lime or lemon

This juice is very high in vitamins, minerals, live enzymes and disease fighting phytochemicals. Watercress is an overlooked liver cleansing spring green that has a spicy punch. Beets are simply the most cleansing, detoxifying and liver rejuvenating food on the planet. Carrots are cleansing and add a nice sweet flavor to the juice. To all you juicing newcomers, this juice is very detoxifying, so be sure to start by drinking only small amounts (three ounces).

CHAPTER FOURTEEN

THE FOUR WINDS HOLISTIC CLEANSE PROGRAM

You have now been thoroughly educated on the history of natural healing, why one should cleanse, new research on toxins, the detox diet and what to expect. Much of the major detoxifying effects of the Four Winds Holistic Cleanse are stimulated by a specific combination of amazing supplements and herbal formulas. These supplements are chosen because they create a specific healing and metabolic change in the body. These particular supplements have also been chosen because they are widely available at health food stores or online (please see the appendix at the back of the book for reliable resources to purchase the recommended cleansing supplements), are safe for a wide variety of people, and are made by companies that meet pharmaceutical standards in manufacturing. I have also personally tested all the supplements on myself and in my clinical work.

You will notice that only herbal supplements are used and no nutritional supplements or prescription medications. The reason is very clear – herbs have been used exclusively as medicine and for cleansing programs for over 2,000 years. Many nutritional supplements have only become popular or researched in the last ten years. In fact, some so-called cleansing nutritional supplements sold today have an unproven safety record. I will always take 2,000 years of documentation and thousands of clinical practitioners' experience over individuals in a lab. Many of the nutritional supplements for sale are more about marketing than actual scientific or clinical research.

Please note there is an option of using liquid extracts or capsules for each formula. The liquid extracts are more concentrated and are more effective. However, they contain a small amount of alcohol as a preservative. Capsules are a better choice for people who can't have any alcohol (such as recovering alcoholics) or those who can't stand the taste of liquids. Liquids can also be taken in warm water to make the taste more palatable.

FOUR WINDS
HOLISTIC CLEANSE PROGRAM

PHASE I – WARM UP CLEANSE

Days 1 Through 7
Begin following the Four Winds Holistic Cleanse Diet. Eat only whole foods in their pure state and those foods on the approved list. Make sure to avoid everything not on the list.

Start incorporating some of the cleansing lifestyle changes and home spa treatments in the following chapter.

- **Begin Taking Liver Cleansing Formula**
  Choose One of the Following:
    - Planetary Formulas Brand: Bupleurum Liver Cleanse
        - 1 tablet, 3 times daily with meals
    - Herbalist & Alchemist Brand: Thistles Compound
        - 40 - 60 drops, 3 times daily with meals
    - Gaia Herbs Brand: Milk Thistle Yellow Dock Supreme
        - 40 - 60 drops, 3 times daily with meals
    - Natures Way Brand: Super Thisilyn
        - 1 capsule, 3 times daily with meals

- **Begin Taking Deep Tissue Alterative Formula**
  Choose One of the Following:

- o Herbalist & Alchemist Brand: Alterative Compound
  - ▪ 40 - 60 drops, 3 times daily
- o Gaia Herbs Brand: Hoxsey Red Clover Supreme
  - ▪ 40 - 60 drops, 3 times daily
- o Planetary Formulas Brand: Red Clover Cleanser
  - ▪ 1 tablet, 3 times daily
- o Gaia Herbs Brand: Cleanse Maintenance
  - ▪ 1 capsule, 3 times daily

- **Optional - Take Lower Bowel Cleansing Formula Choose One of the Following:**
  - o **Only take this product if you are having only one or less bowel movments daily!**
  - o Herbalist & Alchemist Brand: Gentle Lax
    - ▪ 30 drops, 2 times daily
  - o Solaray Brand: Rhubarb & Butternut
    - ▪ 1 capsule, 2 times daily
  - o Nature's Way Brand: Naturalax 2
    - ▪ 1 capsule, 2 times daily
      - • NOTE: If you have excessive loose stools or cramps, discontinue Lower Bowel Cleansing Formula. If you are having two or more bowel movements per day, there is no need to take the Lower Bowel Cleansing Formula at all during the cleanse.

- **Begin Taking Triphala Internal Cleanser Choose One of the Following:**
  - o Planetary Formulas Brand: Triphala Gold
    - ▪ 2 tablets/capsules, 2 times daily
  - o Banyan Botanicals Brand: Triphala
    - ▪ 2 tablets, 2 times daily
  - o Nature's Way Brand: Triphala
    - ▪ 1 capsule, 3 times daily

- **Fiber Formula**

Choose One of the Following:

- o Yerba Prima Brand: Daily Fiber Caps
    - 3 capsules, 2 times daily with lots of warm water
- o Source Naturals Brand: Grapefruit Pectin
    - 3 tablets, 2 times daily with lots of warm water
- o Twinlab Brand: Apple Pectin Caps
    - 3 capsules, 2 times daily with lots of warm water
- o Ground Flax Seeds: 1 tbl, 2 times daily with lots of warm water
- o Any brand of high quality fiber can be used, just make sure it provides 5-10 grams of fiber daily. Mix all fiber with lots of warm water.

Day 7 – Night Before Bed

- If you are not having one or two good bowel movements daily, take one single extra dosage of the Lower Bowel Cleansing Formula before bed.

PHASE II – INTENSE

Day 8 – Juice Fast

- On the eighth day, do a complete juice fast using organic vegetable juices. Beet and carrot juices are considered the best. Fruit juices that are on the diet list are acceptable also. Drink about 3-5 cups per day.
    - o You can also do an organic vegetable broth fast or water fast instead of a juice fast. See modifications below.
    - o You can also use the Four Winds Holistic Cleanse Juice Recipe in the previous chapter.
- If you are diabetic or hypoglycemic, you can do the beans and rice cleansing recipe called kitchari instead of juice fasting. See description below.

- Continue taking all the cleansing supplements and formulas at the same dosages.

PHASE III – COOL DOWN

Day 9 Through 14

- Return to eating only foods on the Four Winds Holistic Cleanse Diet.
- Continue taking all the cleansing supplements and formulas at the same dosages.
  - o If you feel like you are not having many cleansing reactions or you are not having two bowel movements daily, take an extra dose of your Lower Bowel Cleansing Formula.

Day 15 – Transition Off the Cleanse

- Continue eating a healthy whole foods diet emphasizing as many of the foods and diet suggestions from the Four Winds Holistic Cleanse Diet.
- *Slowly go back to eating regular foods.* No oily, greasy or fried foods for a while. Since your liver has been detoxified, it will be very reactive to these heavier foods.
- See the list in Chapter 15 for the Twelve Foundations for Maintaining Daily Detox. These are all great daily changes you can make to encourage gentle, daily detox.

MODIFYING THE PHASE II JUICE FASTING FOR SPECIAL NEEDS

Modification One for Diabetics If you are diabetic or have blood sugar imbalances, you cannot do a juice or broth fast at all. Instead, you should eat kitchari all day on the eighth day. Kitchari is an ancient, bland tasting Ayurvedic deep tissue cleanse recipe of beans, spices and rice. If you notice your blood sugar levels are low, you can add more protein to your diet such as fish, beans, nuts or seeds. If you are still having high or low blood sugar with kitchari, then you should return to eating whole foods from the Four Winds Holistic Cleanse Diet and skip the fast all together.

FOUR WINDS KITCHARI RECIPE

Ingredients
Basmati rice – one cup
mung dahl (split yellow beans)
two cups, water
one half tbs or less, salt
one pinch, ghee (clarified butter)
two tbs, mustard seeds
two tbs, cumin powder
two tsp, turmeric root powder
two tsp, coriander powder
two tsp, fennel powder
two tsp, ginger root powder

Directions
Wash rice and beans thoroughly. Cook the rice separately in two cups of water until fully done. In a separate pan, lightly sauté mustard seeds in the ghee until they snap. Add all the other spices. Add the mung dahl and salt. Lightly cook for about two minutes. Add five cups of water and bring to boil. Simmer covered for 50 minutes or until the dahl is fully cooked. It should have a soupy appearance. Keep checking and stir regularly. Serve the dahl soupy mixture over top of the basmati rice. You can add other steamed vegetables on the side also.

Modification Two for Those Who Can't Do Juices If you don't want to do vegetable juices on day eight of fasting, you can eat organic vegetable broth all day. (It is not as healing or detoxifying as vegetable juices.) Just make sure the broth you use is yeast free. Other people find only drinking water all day on day eight is easier on their body.

Modification Three for Cancer Patients If you are very weak or have a chronic illness such as cancer, you can add some protein to your diet during both the cleanse and juice fast. Add a high quality whey protein powder (without artificial colors, sweeteners or aspartame) to your cleansing diet. Whey protein can be mixed with water or almond milk.

What If Your Cleanse Is Not Doing Much?

First, remember cleansing is more than just more frequent bowel movements. Observe all the array of cleansing symptoms from earlier chapters. Most people only have three or five symptoms of cleansing at once. If you are doing the cleanse and still not experiencing much change, then add an extra dosage of your liver cleanse formula, deep tissue alterative formula and lower bowel cleansing formula. (It usually doesn't help to add more fiber or triphala.) You can also be more restrictive with your diet and add more home spa therapies.

It is important for everyone to remember that there will be different experiences each cleanse. In general, the first three cleanses will be the most detoxifying because the body is not used to it and you have a lot of old "crap" stored up. One of your first three cleanses will usually be very intense, while the other two will be mild. After completing a third FWH Cleanse, most people notice they have a less dramatic cleansing experience in the future. This is good because it shows those toxins are being removed from the deep tissues and organs of the body.

Advanced Cleansers

After you have completed the FWH Cleanse at least four times, you may want to make some modifications. The natural tendency for patients is to say, "That cleanse was great, but I want to go even deeper this season." First, advanced cleansers can add an extra dosage of their liver cleansing formula, deep tissue alterative formula and lower bowel cleansing formula. Second, you can try occasionally skipping a meal and having a cleansing vegetable juice instead. Third, you can keep doing all your cleansing formulas and supplements – except the Lower Bowel Cleanse Formula – for another week after the cleanse is over. (The Lower Bowel Cleanse Formula should not be used for more than two weeks.) Fourth, you can try a two or three day juice fast for deeper detox. This can be done by juice fasting on days seven, eight and nine.

For those of you with years of experience, be advised you will periodically have one difficult cleanse every three years. I am not exactly sure why this happens in three year cycles, but it does. People will often notice different cleansing experiences each year. One year more emotions may be released. One year more skin problems are prominent, one year more digestive changes are noticed. Other years there may be more muscle aches and cold like symptoms. This is just the body expressing its intelligence and focusing on one weak area of your body at a time.

CLEANSING TIPS

Kitchari can be eaten at any time to appease the appetite during the juice fast. A few people will feel better by adding more protein during their cleanse. You can simply eat more fish, nuts, seeds and beans. If you have severe gallbladder attacks, stop the herbal formulas until the pain subsides. Slowly add back formulas, as long as there is no pain. If you are having more than three bowel movements daily or lots of digestive cramping, simply quit taking the Lower Bowel Cleansing Formula for two days. You may not experience more than one bowel movement during your juice fast. This is normal because you are restricting food and fiber intake.

ACCESSORY CLEANSING PRODUCTS

The FWH Cleanse Program is totally complete. However, experienced cleansers may benefit by adding additional products to increase the effectiveness of their program. The following is a list of helpful natural products my patients have enjoyed while cleansing:

- Fasting Tea by the Yogi company is very helpful for appetite cravings during any cleansing diet. The dosage is one cup, two or three times daily.
- Green food drinks like barely grass, wheat grass, spirulina and chlorella, can be consumed throughout the cleanse for additional benefit. Many people are allergic to grasses and can have reactions to wheat or barley grass. If you feel like you are having allergic reactions such as runny nose, sniffling, sneezing or mucus, don't use these particular products.

- Dandelion root tea or nettle leaf tea, commonly used in European detox clinics, can be consumed throughout the entire cleanse for additional benefit.
- Ginger root tea can help to raise body temperature and help control the appetite while cleansing.
- Ayurvedic Chyvanaprash is an ancient cleansing formula that can be consumed by anyone. It can be obtained from Banyan Botanicals (see resource section). If you have cancer, you may want to consider using this product long term as it has been shown to have many supportive effects for cancer patients.

TROUBLE SHOOTING FOR COMMON CLEANSING PROBLEMS

The Four Winds Holistic Cleanse is designed to be safe and will work for almost everyone. There are some common problems that may arise which can be easily resolved with simple changes. If you experience a combination of unbearable cleansing symptoms (as discussed earlier), you should simply stop taking all the cleansing supplements for a day. Continue taking the fiber supplement and continue on the diet. In almost every case, all cleansing symptoms go away. The next day when you feel better, start the cleansing supplements again at half the recommended dosage for a day. If you don't feel better the next day, still hold off taking the cleansing supplements until you feel better.

CONSTIPATION

You should have one to three bowel movements daily while cleansing. If you are having less than one bowel movement daily, simply take an additional dosage of your Bowel Cleansing Herbal Formula and drink an extra glass of water daily. Remember that during your juice fast, there may be no bowel movements the next day because you are not eating any fiber.

LIVER PAIN AND GALLBLADDER SPASMS

If you have liver or gallbladder spasms that are painful, temporarily stop your Liver Cleansing Herbal Formula for a day. Keep taking all your other supplements and stay on the cleansing diet. If the pain subsides in a day, start all your Liver Cleansing Herbal Formula at half the recommended dosage. Then, go back up to regular dosage the following day. If you still have pain, don't start the Liver Cleansing Herbal Formula until the liver pain is gone.

EXTREME DIARRHEA OR INTESTINAL CRAMPING

If you experience excessive diarrhea or painful bowel movements, quit taking your Lower Bowel Cleansing Formula for a day. If the diarrhea subsides, then start the formula again at half the dosage the next day. If you are having two or three bowel movements daily, then simply stay at that dosage during your cleanse.

LOWER BACK AND KIDNEY ACHES

If you have extremely painful lower back or kidney pains, stop all your cleansing herbal formulas for a day. Continue on the diet and keep taking the fiber supplement. Also drink an extra glass of water each day. If the pain subsides in a day, start all your herbal cleansing formulas at half dosage for a day.

PURCHASING CLEANSING PRODUCTS

All products, supplements and herbal formulas used in the Four Winds Holistic Cleanse can be purchased at a local health food store or at the authors website www.cleansingdepot.com.

CHAPTER FIFTEEN

CLEANSING LIFESTYLE CHANGES & DETOX HOME SPA TREATMENTS

It is important to again emphasize the Four Winds Holistic Cleanse is a complete system. There are a variety of other lifestyle changes and home spa treatments you can utilize to make the cleanse much more detoxifying. If you are really motivated, or if you have a chronic disease you want to heal, you should try adding as many of these additional treatments as you can while following the two week cleanse. Most of them cost little money and can be done from the comfort of your home. Since you can't do all of these additional recommendations, try choosing the ones that sound the most fun and relaxing to you!

Holistic cleansing is a math equation. Imagine you are trying to add up to a score of a hundred points. The supplements, diet and lifestyle recommendations are each 25 points. Maybe you are under great stress, so there is a minus of 15 points. Maybe you still have a cup of coffee everyday and another 10 points are lost. (It is important to note that any herbal teas including green or black should not be consumed while on the cleanse. You are already getting enough herb power from the supplements and we don't want to confuse or overwhelm the body with these additions.) All of these accessory treatments are a great way to "add points" to your cleansing goal of deepest detox possible. They are useful for any season. The more home spa treatments you add, the more you will transform you body.

One of the goals of the FWH Cleanse is to make lasting lifestyle and dietary changes which you maintain after the cleanse. Most people are shocked to find out how bad their diet really is or how many toxic compounds are in their house. These changes can help to create a more green and non-toxic lifestyle for your family.

FOUR WINDS HOLISTIC CLEANSE HOME SPA TREATMENTS

Take an Epsom salt bath Epsom salts help to pull toxins out of our skin and deep tissues. They are also an old, time proven home remedy for muscle aches and pains. Epsom salts are mineral crystals that make the water closer to how a natural spring would be. Simply place two cups of Epsom salts into a tub of hot bath water. You can often find many aromatherapy bath blends that have sea salt and Epsom salts in them. These are available at any health food store.

Get a lymphatic or deep tissue massage Deep tissue massage and lymphatic massages are a specialty of some massage therapists. Any massage would be healing during the cleanse because it helps to release stored toxins from the deep tissues of the body. Massage will also help to reduce stress levels, improve circulation and stimulate the body's innate healing response. Deep tissue and lymphatic massages may be a little more painful than the common Swedish massage. Remember, "No pain, no gain!"

Receive a Traditional Chinese or Mayan abdominal massage Abdominal massage, often called chi nei tsang, is practiced by some acupuncturists and those trained in Oriental massage (tuina). The practitioner gently massages all the internal organs through the abdomen, thereby releasing stored emotions and toxins in the tissues. Since it facilitates the movement of blood into the pelvic cavity, women with uterine or ovarian issues often find this type of massage helpful.

Sit in a hot sauna Sweating is one of the original forms of natural healing that goes back as far as records can trace. In many countries of the world, saunas are still used as part of their healthcare system. There are hundreds of medical research studies on the health benefits of saunas. Sweating stimulates detox at all levels of the body. Saunas have been shown to help stimulate detox, relax muscles, stimulate the immune system, balance hormonal disorders, increase the excretion of wastes/toxins, increase metabolism, treat sinus and respiratory tract infections and assist with water retention. They have hundreds of other healing properties. It is interesting that almost every traditional culture around the world has some type of steam healing ceremony. The most common would be the sweat lodges of the Native Americans or the Scandinavians. You can take one or two saunas per week while cleansing. You can buy day passes to many gyms that have saunas.

Have a mud wrap or seaweed wrap Mud wraps and seaweed wraps are very cleansing. They can help draw toxins and pollutants out of our skin. You don't have to pay lots of money for these wraps. You can often buy these treatments from health food stores, online from a spa supplier or you can make your own. They are a little messy though.

Meditation and deep breathing There are at least 750 scientific studies showing the health benefits of meditation and deep breathing. These two simple methods help stimulate detox by allowing the nervous, endocrine and immune systems to come into a state of calmness. Relaxation stimulates the metabolic pathways of cell regeneration. Deep breathing has been shown to stimulate the excretion of waste and toxins by stimulating all the cells with a super charged dose of oxygen.

Don't feel like you have to burn incense or chant or sit in painful postures to meditate. For those of you who are new to meditation, the goal is that you are relaxed and have a calm mind. Many patients find that relaxation tapes and music work well. There are a variety of guided relaxation tapes you can buy at any bookstore. For those of you who want to study meditation deeper, many community centers have free meditation classes. There are also thousands of books written on the topic. Fifteen to thirty minutes a day is all it takes.

Start a personal journal Many patients have found journaling to be a great way to release all the emotions and worries they have. Many of my patients have found it is a great way to reflect back on their healing journey. The FWH Cleanse addresses the need to release toxic emotions and negative thoughts that prevent the healing process. It is amazing that simply writing down how you feel can have a deep healing effect on your body.

Share three hugs daily Hugs might not be researched to stimulate cleansing, but there is plenty of scientific research to show their healing effects on the body and mind. Hugs can come from animals, too.

Spend quality time with family Spending time with family and loved ones is not detoxifying to the body, but it is healing to the mind and emotions. The FWH Cleanse addresses the importance of healing our mental and spiritual bodies also. There is an old Native American teaching that true health cannot be achieved until one has overcome all family emotional issues. I see patients every week who still struggle with strained relationships with family members. You may not be able to heal all those past hurts, but it is vital to recognize they may be affecting your health.

Avoid or dramatically reduce TV time TV is one of the worst disruptors of our nervous system and mood. People are amazed at how emotionally balanced they are by reducing TV time. Watching TV or staring at computer screens all day long really agitates our nervous system and mind. I have seen lots of patients who significantly reduced their stress level of their life by simply turning off their TVs and reading a book. Remember, natural healing is simple. Scientists have now proven that TVs and computers emit electromagnetic radiation. We don't yet understand the long-term health consequences of being around these devices all day.

Swim in a lake or natural stream There is something inherently powerful about swimming in a natural stream or lake. Just make sure it is not polluted. The Greeks and Romans cherished the healing powers of water. Remember how good you felt after being on the lake all day as a child? I am amazed that most people live around pristine lakes and waters, yet they never swim in them. Again we see how natural healing is both fun and effortless.

Spend time in Nature Every healing process requires nature. The best way to stimulate healing is to foster your connection to nature by being outside. Many patients have been amazed at how spending one day each week in nature can alleviate stress, improve sense of well being and help fight depression. Remember that healing happens from lots of small changes that add up.

During the cleanse, it is important to be in nature and observe nature. It allows you to see how you are affected by the season changes, weather and all of nature's cycles. We live in isolated square boxes today called houses. People think they are isolated from the effects or cycles of nature, but our bodies and minds still follow these internal patterns. Whether it is seasonal allergies, or the effects of Seasonal Affective Disorder in fall, weather affects us all. We all are part of nature and change with it. Having a nice outdoor picnic with family or friends is a great way to get outside. Be sure to bring a blanket and actually sit on the earth itself. Take a small nap and lay on your back looking up at the sun. I know one patient who spends his juice fasting day picking up trash at local lakes. Get outside to hike, walk, bicycle or camp.

Do dry skin brushing This is a traditional detox method heavily favored by practitioners of Ayurvedic medicine. It is best to perform dry skin brushing each morning before showering or working out. Patients are amazed at how energizing it is. Dry skin brushing stimulates the flow of lymphatic fluids, circulation and the deep tissues of the body. As I stressed earlier, the skin is a major organ of detox that should not be overlooked in holistic cleansing.

You can use a loofah sponge, skin brush, shower brush or special dry mitten. Many of these brushes can be purchased at health food or bath products stores. The traditional routine is to start at your hands and brush towards your heart. Then do both feet, brushing towards your heart. Next do the abdomen in clockwise circles. Finally brush your scalp, neck and face. This is particularly good for larger build body types, people who retain water, anyone with poor circulation and those with a history of tumors or cysts. A few scientific studies have found dry skin brushing can help break up unsightly cellulite.

Walk barefoot in nature Take those shoes off, especially those of you who never let your feet breathe! Take off as much of your clothes as you can without getting in trouble of course! Your skin is a major organ of detox. Let your skin breathe for once. Let your feet and body absorb the healing effects of sunlight and fresh air. The famous early American herbalist, Dr. John Christopher, recommended his patients walk outside on the grass each morning while it was covered in dew, and many healers throughout time have agreed with him. It is truly an invigorating experience.

Positive visualizations Take time daily to visualize whatever parts of your body need healing. For example, if you have liver problems, see the liver completely regenerating. If you have cancer, see your immune system killing off all cancer cells or see tumors shrinking. If you want to focus on cleansing, see all the toxins being released from your body. See every cell of your body transforming into a bright yellow new vibrant cells. Most patients feel this exercise is best done during or after relaxation time or during meditation.

Switch to natural cosmetics Some research has shown that commercial cosmetics contain up to 200 known toxins! Shampoos, conditioners, deodorants, makeup, hair gel and hair spray all contain known toxins. Adding all those toxins on a daily basis can really add up. Try switching to an all natural or organic cosmetics line.

Try a castor oil pack on your liver Castor oil packs can be done to help stimulate detox and the release of toxins. Simply massage castor oil on your liver area (right hemisphere of your body) near the ribcage down to the waist. Place a damp towel over it and place a heating pad on top. Let it sit for 30 minutes and then rub off any remaining castor oil. If you have never tried castor oil packs, don't do them before work. They can cause quick detox symptoms and mild cramps. Adding a few drops of the essential oils of rosemary, lemon, cypress or pine will have additional cleansing effects.

Start a tai chi or chi kung class Tai chi and chi kung are two ancient Chinese health practices that are hundreds of years old. There is a tremendous amount of research showing how these two practices can help reverse disease, detoxify the body, strengthen the immune system and adrenal glands, balance hormones, improve coordination and balance, calm the nervous system, reduce the side effects of radiation and chemotherapy and much more. I advise every patient to start either yoga, tai chi or chi kung practice. There is no better way to rejuvenate the body and promote longevity. Why do you think there are so many older healthy people doing tai chi in the park?

The best tai chi and chi kung videos can be purchased from Master Chen. He teaches authentic styles and I have personally studied with him. His videos and relaxation CDs are the best available if you do not have a teacher in your community. I recommend his Tai Chi Chi Kung 18 Forms and/or the Primordial Chi Kung DVDs. They can be purchased on his website at www.wudangtao.com or from other resources listed in the appendix of the book.

Detox Herbal Steam Baths

Herbal baths and detox steam baths are one of the oldest healing methods known to man. The Greeks, Egyptians, Romans, Mayans, Aztecs and most Native Americans had some form of steam bath or sauna. These baths were used for cleansing, ceremonies and healing. Herbal baths are still used today by herbalists and physicians around the world to treat a variety of diseases.

Herbal steam baths should be used at least once every week as you are cleansing. It is best to set a goal of three steam baths or hot dry saunas each week during your cleanse. It is important to not do steam baths any more than that because they can create electrolyte imbalances. When you get out of the bath, you will be red from head to toe!

A good detox bath has four aspects: hot water, steam, herbs and Epsom salts. The Epsom salts help to draw toxins out of the skin and lymphatic system. It also helps to relax the muscles and prevent electrolyte imbalances. The hot water induces sweating, stimulating our bodies to release toxins. The herbs penetrate the skin and into the deeper tissues to stimulate the cleansing response. The steam opens our pores and also assists in detoxifying the lungs, head and sinuses.

First you have to prepare the herbal tea for the bath. You will have to buy most of these herbs at the health food store or online. All the herbs should be purchased as dried cut herbs (called cut and sifted) except for ginger which can also be powdered. The most common herbs added to baths are rosemary herb, sage leaf, basil herb, lavender flower, linden flower, yarrow flower, red clover flower, peppermint leaf, ginger root and elder flower.

The following is an herbal bath recipe I have used with patients for many years. Don't stress if you can't get all the herbs; just use as many as you can. Place all the herbs in one gallon of water in large pot on the stove. Bring to a near boil, remove from heat and cover with a lid. Let it sit for five minutes. Pour this mixture into the bottom of your bathtub through a pasta strainer. Fill up the rest of the tub with hot water, as hot as you can stand! Pour in two cups of Epsom salts. Stir well to dissolve.

Four Winds Detox Steam Bath

Herb	Amount	Detox Function
Ginger Root	2 tbl	Ginger baths deeply invigorate circulation and allow the bath to have a deeper detox response in the body.
Yarrow Flower	3 tbl	Induces a deep sweating response and opens the pores.
Elder Flower	2 tbl	Induces a deep sweating response and opens the pores.
Sage Leaf	1 tbl	A very purifying and cleansing herb that also opens the pores. Helps to balance emotions and negative thoughts.
Linden Flower	1 tbl	Induces deep sweating, stimulates the immune system and has a very calming effect. Very good for helping with heart and circulations problems.
Basil Herb	1 tbl	A major component of traditional South American healing baths.

You should sit in the tub for about 15-20 minutes. The bathroom should be totally closed off so there are no cold drafts and the steam keeps building up. Drink plenty of room temperature water while you are in the tub. If you feel light headed or dizzy, then slowly get out of the tub.

You don't want to overheat. You are not trying to cook yourself like a turkey! You are trying to increase your body temperature enough to promote detox and healing of the immune system. If you are sensitive to heat, then keep a cool towel on your neck or cover your head with it, so that you can still sweat out the toxins.

You're not done yet! Ideally, as soon as you get out of the shower, you should do a contrast shower. Turn on the shower as cold as you can tolerate. Let the water hit your entire body. You only need to do this for about 30-60 seconds. This practice has been done for thousands of years. In the Native American sweat lodge, people would jump into a cold lake or stream afterwards, even in the winter. In Scandinavian countries, they jump into the snow after their hot sauna. Contrast showers have been shown in scientific studies to provide a number of health benefits including immune system changes, neurological changes and circulation changes. Plus its fun. In the cold Nebraska snowy winters I like to have a hot sauna, jump into the snow for about 15 seconds, then go back and sit in the sauna. There is nothing like it.

ENEMAS

Enemas are a hot topic in natural healthcare as they have been regaining the popularity they once held in the 1970s. The history of enemas for detox and health date back to some of the first writings on natural healing. The oldest references include papyrus medical scrolls detailing how over two thousand years ago, ancient Egyptian doctors used enemas with herbs and pure river water to heal many diseases. The history then traces through ancient Greece and Roman times and into Europe, where it has been part of the traditional healing arts for many years.

COLONICS VERSUS ENEMAS

Enemas are very, very mild in nature and don't stress the bowels when used only occasionally. Colonics are aggressive and can aggravate the intestinal lining in sensitive people, almost like a car wash for your enema. Enemas are preferred for anyone who has had a history of intestinal problems or has a sensitive system. Remember that the FWH Cleanse is based on time tested traditional practices that have been shown to be safe for hundreds of years. Colonics are a recent practice and were not part of any traditional cleansing system.

HEALTH PRECAUTIONS WITH ENEMAS

Those with lower bowel diseases should consult a healthcare provider before trying enemas. Enemas should only be used sporadically, as they can cause bowel dependency. I have had many patients who became dependent upon multiple enemas weekly to have normal bowel movements. The purpose of enemas is to stimulate a deeper cleanse of the lining of the intestinal wall, removing pockets of debris and accumulation.

HOW OFTEN TO USE ENEMAS WITH YOUR CLEANSE

The most effective way to use enemas is to do a single enema during your juice fast phase of cleansing on day eight. Enemas help assist the body by going into a deeper cleansing state. There is no need to do more than one or two enemas per week while on the cleanse program. No one should feel like they need enemas. If the idea is foreign or stressful to you, then there is no need to use them. They are just one of the many accessory healing practices you can choose from in this chapter. If you do choose a colonic, there is no need to do more than one during the whole two week cleanse.

WHAT TYPE OF ENEMAS?

There is great confusion in America as what is best to add to the enema. Unfortunately, most people only use coffee enemas. I do not support using coffee enemas because they work by irritating the nerves of the large intestine. What type of enema is best? After years of working with patients, I have created a very mild cleansing enema that doesn't irritate the lining or nerves of the colon. Like the herbal steam bath, try to get as many of the herbs as possible but don't stress out if you can't get them all. If you don't have access to any of these herbs, then you can do a regular warm water enema with four tablespoons of sesame oil added to it.

FOUR WINDS HOLISTIC CLEANSE ENEMA

Ingredients
Burdock Root – 1 tbl
Yellow Dock Root – 1 tbl
Red Clover Flower – 1 tbl
Dandelion Root – 1 tbl
Catnip Herb – 1 tbl
Sesame Seed Oil – 2 tbl

Directions
All herbs should be purchased as dried cut or whole herbs. No powders! Place all herbs in a stainless steel pot. Cover with six cups of water. Bring to a boil. Cover and place on low heat for thirty minutes. Strain in pasta strainer. Let cool to room temperature before using as enema. Enema kits can be purchased at any pharmacy or online from an herbalist supply warehouse.

OTHER ADDITIONAL HELPFUL RECOMMENDATIONS

- Pray/meditate/visualize your body releasing old toxins and replacing diseased tissues.
- Focus on new beginnings in all aspects of your life, including new goals, dreams, and aspirations.
- Embrace some type of creative expression – writing, poetry, art, dance, exercise, talking, etc. Let go of old emotions like anger, resentment and frustration.
- Clear all the clutter out of your house or read about Feng Shui. Clean your house by removing old junk you don't need and donating it to the poor or needy. Cleaning is a very symbolic act of purging all that is old and useless to stimulate new growth. This is a very symbolic gesture of letting go and moving on with your life.
- Clean your house with natural cleaning products. Don't use household toxic cleaners, bug sprays and dangerous cleaning chemicals on your cleanse. Using these toxic cleaners defeats everything you are doing internally. If you can smell it or feel it on your skin, it is in your body. Try shopping at a health

food store for your home cleaning products.
- Help the body by doing some light exercise such as t'ai chi, yoga or walking.
- Dress warm in layers, as the cleanse will lower your body temperature.

NOTE: Look at the Resources section for supplements and cleansing supplies in the appendix of this book.

ULTIMATE FOUR WINDS
HOLISTIC CLEANSE HOME SPA

You don't have to pay thousands of dollars to go to a fancy health spa during your cleanse. You can do almost everything you need to do at home. The following is a cost effective home spa system I developed for patients to use at home during their cleanse. It incorporates almost all the modalities described earlier.

- Take a vigorous outdoor hike. Come home and put on some relaxing music and light some candles. Use some relaxing aromatherapy product like a scented candle or incense. Good relaxing aromatherapy oils during a cleanse are lavender, clary sage, geranium, rose and ylang ylang.
- Get a deep tissue massage. The massage can be from a professional or from a friend.
- Take an herbal enema.
- Do five minutes of vigorous skin brushing with a skin brush.
- Sit in an herbal steam detox bath or sauna. When done with the hot bath, take a cold contrast shower.
- Smudge yourself or burn some white sage, sagebrush or sweet grass.
- Put on some warm relaxing clothes.
- Have a nice cleansing meal over candlelight.
- Before bed, give yourself a warm scalp oil massage. Heat up sesame oil so it is warm. Massage the warm sesame oil deeply into all of your scalp. Wrap your head in a towel and have the deepest sleep ever!

- Go to bed early and wake up late. Even the most expensive spas in the world can't compare to this.

OTHER LIFESTYLE CONSIDERATIONS DURING THE CLEANSE

The Four Winds Holistic Cleanse focuses the body's energies and resources on detoxification. We want to make sure the body's resources are not being devoted to other processes. Extremely strenuous workouts with weights or working out for excessively long periods of time are not advised while cleansing. The excessive exercising pushes the body into a more catabolic (breakdown) state. Gentle exercise like yoga, stretching, walking in nature and t'ai chi are the best. These are very rejuvenating systems of exercise that allow the body, mind and spirit to become harmonized. The high amounts of adrenaline and stress hormones released with excessive workouts are very antagonistic to the healing process.

CHAPTER SIXTEEN

AFTER THE CLEANSE

YOUR NEW BODY

Congratulations! After the completion of the Four Winds Holistic Cleanse, your body is in a rejuvenated state. Most of your bodily systems are functioning at a dramatically more effective rate. After the cleanse, your self-healing regulatory systems can better take control of the body again. We often refer to this as spontaneous healing in our profession. If you just give the body what it needs, it will find a way to heal itself. It is exciting to know that your body will be in an increased state of cellular regeneration for up to two weeks after your cleanse is over since the body is still in a healing phase. It is still important to eat very healthily for these additional two weeks after your cleanse.

Bowel movements should still be much more regular than before. Many in western healthcare think that constipation is when you don't have a bowel movement for more than five days. I remember working in the hospital as a nutritionist and reading notes by doctors or nurses that a patient hadn't had a bowel movement in seven days. They were concerned the patient might develop constipation. Everyone should have one to two bowel movements per day.

Most patients experience anywhere from five to ten pounds of safe weight loss after the completion of their cleanse. I have had patients who lost up to 25 pounds after one month of advanced, supervised deep tissue cleansing. It is important to know that they felt great the whole time because the diet is so healthy and nourishing.

Holistic cleansing is one of the best ways to overcome chronic allergies. I have had countless patients notice that their allergies lessoned 15-25% after each cleanse. Over the course of a few years, patients are usually mostly allergy free. I have witnessed many patients go off of allergy medications, sinus sprays and inhalers after a few years of following the FWH Cleanse once every season.

There are many other signs you may notice which indicate your body is now rejuvenating. They include a few of the following: fingernails and hair will grow rapidly; an increased sense of energy, vitality, sexual drive; improved digestion, less acidity, more bowel regularity; clearer skin; improved hormone balance, increased fertility with women; stronger immune system; greater emotional balance; higher spiritual inspiration and an improved sense of mood.

POST CLEANSE REBOUND EFFECT

There is a common occurrence many people have after their cleanse which I refer to as the Post Cleanse Rebound Effect. About 20% of all people who finish the cleanse will experience this. The Post Cleanse Rebound Effect is the experience your body has healed, and it can now better express to you what foods it doesn't want. Common experiences are constipation, sensitivity to environmental toxins, nausea and increased digestive reactions to unhealthy or allergic foods. Many refer to it as the "cleansing curse," but it is far from that. Your body is telling you exactly which foods you may be allergic to or that are unhealthy to eat. Constipation is more common because most people return to a lower fiber diet. If this occurs, try to avoid the offending foods and simply add more fiber and water to your diet.

Your reactivity to environmental toxins is the body telling you to stop. Do not go to smoky bars right during or after a cleanse. You will likely get very ill and have strong reactions to the smoke. Also, do not consume large amounts of alcohol right after the cleanse or you will get sick. You will notice a very low alcohol tolerance for quite some time after the cleanse. For example, if you normally have three drinks, then you would likely feel almost drunk after one or two drinks. You may even feel different allergic-like reactions to over the counter medications.

What You Can Do to Maintain Detox After the Cleanse

What about after the big cleanse? We should not abandon our pursuit of health, healing and cleansing. It is just as important to maintain a healthy diet and lifestyle after the cleanse. The more we can minimize the toxic overload on our systems, the healthier we will be. As mentioned earlier, this is true with almost all chronic diseases. Over the years, I have created a list of twelve simple changes you can make after your cleanse to minimize toxin exposure and stimulate daily detox.

Twelve Foundations for Maintaining Daily Detox After the Cleanse

ONE

Eat Organically Grown Foods Eating organic is one of the simplest ways to reduce your toxin intake and improve the nutritional value of the food you eat. You not only decrease toxic intake, but you also support farming that is not making the problems worse. We could all eat healthy, but if our environment gets much more polluted, we will be in major trouble.

TWO

Follow a Whole Food Diet Try to follow the principles of the cleansing diet and incorporating more whole foods on a daily basis. Focus on eating all foods in their whole, pure, fresh and unprocessed state. Avoid all processed foods and fast food as much as possible. Simply reading the ingredient lists of fast foods, one can see there is little nutritional value or freshness in most of the foods they sell.

THREE

Spend Time in Nature Each Week Remember our statement, "All healing requires nature!" Return to nature to nourish yourself. Spending time in nature heals the body, calms the emotions and revitalizes the spirit. It's free too!

FOUR

Relax Simply put, stress kills. Stress has been linked with almost every known disease in humans. Do whatever it takes to learn to relax and limit your reactions to stress. Everyone has stress in their life; some people just react to it more. Don't play the victim by always saying you have more stress than anyone else. Solve the problem and proactively reduce your reaction to stress.

FIVE

Take a Milk Thistle Supplement Milk thistle seed supplements can be taken safely for long periods of time between cleanses. It helps to protect the liver from toxins and gently assist in the removal of waste. It has also been shown to stimulate the growth of new liver cells. Many of the companies listed in the resource section of the appendix carry a high quality milk thistle supplement.

SIX

Take a Fiber Supplement Fiber supplements are a great way to maintain digestive health, support detox and lower cholesterol.

SEVEN

Take a Multivitamin and Mineral Daily Buy your vitamins at a health food store because most sold at drug stores and department stores are filled with fillers, binders, coloring agents, coatings and synthetic Vitamin E. Most people only need a simple once daily formula with antioxidants. The emphasis should be on eating healthy, organic, whole foods first. Men should always take an iron free supplement.

EIGHT

Switch to Green Home Products A "green home" is essential to health. You can cleanse all you want, but if you keep polluting your house with toxic chemicals, you will always struggle with health. The following are some of the more important products to stop using: paints, varnishes, wood/deck stains, bug sprays, insecticides, synthetic lawn fertilizers, lawn/gardening chemicals, sanitizing sprays, bath tub cleaners, tile and countertop cleaners, disinfecting sprays and most laundry detergents. Natural alternatives can be found for virtually any product made today. Refer to my website in the resource section for more detailed information on this topic.

NINE

Drink Distilled, Spring or Reverse Osmosis Purified Water Distilled water and spring water are great. Reverse osmosis water is the best because it removes the most toxins from water especially the smaller hormone-like compounds. You can buy very cheap home treatment systems for less than $150. You will save money and the environment. Buying plastic bottles of water consumes lots of petroleum and natural resources for distribution. Most home filtering systems pay for themselves in as little as six months. Check out your local department store or the Giam catalogue (www.giam.com) for a complete list of available models.

TEN

Try Digestive Bitters Before Meals Herbal bitters can be taken before each meal to assist the liver in bile production and stimulate your bodies own digestive enzyme production. Try one of the following bitters formulas:

- Herbalist & Alchemist Brand: Bitters Compound
  - 60 drops, dilluted in one ounce of water, before meals
- Planetary Formulas Brand: Digestive Grape Bitters
  - 1 teaspoon, diluted in one ounce of water, before meals
- Gaia Herbs Brand: Swedish Bitters

    o   60 drops, diluted in one ounce of water, before meals
- This is the only formula that is available as alcohol free

ELEVEN

Support Environmental Causes You don't have to be a hippie to be concerned about the environment. Our Earth is in a great state of crisis. If we take global and corporate pollution much further, no amount of cleansing will help. Saving the Earth is not difficult. If we all would make some simple changes, the whole planet could heal. A few simple solutions include: recycling, buying energy efficient light bulbs, turning off lights when they are not being used, turning down your thermostat by two degrees in the winter, turning up your thermostat two degrees in the summer and donating money to an ecological protection group.

TWELVE

Switch to Natural Cosmetics and Personal Care Products See the discussion in previous chapters on the many toxic potentials of using many commercial cosmetics, shampoos, facial cleansers, hair gels, conditioners and soaps. Again, refer to the resource section in the appendix for a list of suppliers. Most can be found at area health food stores.

CONCLUSION

Parting Thoughts

Embrace the rhythms of nature and seasons of change as you start the Four Winds Holistic Cleanse. I know you will have great rewards revitalizing your entire body, mind and spirit as you embark on your new adventures in cleansing. Embrace the unlimited healing benefits of natural healing. Enjoy creating new dietary and healthy lifestyle changes that will nourish you the rest of your life. Strive to continue living a green lifestyle and understand that every choice you make affects the world around you. Be an inspiration to your family, friends and co-workers by being an example of someone who regained their health through cleansing. Always remember health is our birthright, and diseases merely exist to teach us valuable lessons on the journey of life. Use cleansing as a tool to overcome your own health ailments and empower your life. Come back to who you truly are. Someone with joy, effervesence and health. Enjoy, and happy cleansing!

Resources

Finding Products, Formulas & Supplies for Cleansing

All the products, supplements, teas, books, herbs, massage oils and videos mentioned in this book can be purchased from the author's website. Many articles on cleansing and cleansing recipes can also be found on the website. *www.cleansingdepot.com*

Find a local family owned health food store. Search the National Natural Foods Association website for the location nearest you. *www.naturalproductsassoc.org*

Mountain Rose Herbs. A great small company that stocks all kinds of herbal supplies, especially bulk herbs and essential oils. *www.mountainroseherbs.com*

Finding an Alternative Medicine Practitioner

Locate a nationally accredited clinical herbalist by visiting the American Herbalists Guild website. *www.americanherbalistsguild.org*

Locate a licensed naturopathic doctor by visiting the National Association of Naturopathic Physicians website. *www.naturopathic.org*

Learn authentic Wu Dang Tai Chi, Chi Kung and Kung Fu from a true living master. Go to Master Chen's website for upcoming classes, workshops; China trips and videos. www.wudangtao.com

Locate a licensed acupuncturist and practitioner of Traditional Chinese Medicine by visiting the American Association of Acupuncture and Oriental Medicine website. *www.aaaomonline.org*

Environmental and Green Home Product Sites

Giam Company. A complete array of green home products, water filtration system and green living products. A great source of information on solar panels. *www.Giam.com*

Aubrey Organics. Truly, completely natural hair and skin care products. *www.aubrey-organics.com*

Informative Websites On Natural Healing

The Dangers of Bisphenol A. A website devoted to educating the public on the potential dangers of Bisphenol A. *www.bisphenolafree. org*

Environmental Working Group Website. A complete list of updated research papers detailing the effects of toxins in our environment. All information can be accessed for free and is easy to navigate. Check it out at *www.ewg.org*

REFERENCES

- Agency USEP. Integrated Risk Informational System: Bisphenol A (CASRN 80-05-07). US Environmental Protection Agency; 1998.

- Altman, Nathaniel. *Healing Springs – The Ultimate Guide to Taking the Waters.* Healing Arts Press: Rochester, VT, 2000.

- American Cancer Society. Cancer Facts and figures 2006. Pages 9, 22.

- Bartram, Thomas. *Encyclopedia of Herbal Medicine.* Grace Publishers, Dorset, UK. 1995.

- Blumenthal, M, Goldberg, A, Brinckman, J. *Herbal Medicine: Expanded Commission E Monographs.* Integrative Medicine Communications, Newton, MA. 2000.

- Chiao J, Wu H, Ramaswamy G, et al. Ingestion of an isothiocyanate metabolite from cruciferous vegetables inhibits growth of human prostate cancer cell xenografts by apoptosis and cell cycle arrest. *Carcinogenesis.* 2004 Aug;25(8):1403-08.

- Christopher, John. *School of Natural Healing.* Christopher Publications, Inc.: Springville, UT. 1996.

- Duncan, David Ewing. "The Pollution Within" *National Geographic*, October 2006, pages 116-143.

- Earth Day Organization Website.

- Environmental Working Group Website. www.ewg.org.

- Felter, Harvey. *The Eclectic Materia Medica, Pharmacology & Therapeutics.* Cincinnati, OH. 1922.

- Higdon J, Delage B, Williams D, Dashwood R. Cruciferous vegetables and human cancer risk: epidemiologic evidence and mechanistic basis. *Pharmacol Res.* 2007 Mar; 55(3), 224-236.

- Ho S, Tang W, Belmonte de Frasusto J, Prins G.

Developmental exposure to estradiol and Bisphenol A increases susceptibility to prostate carcinogenesis and epigenetically regulates phosphodiesterase type 4 cariant 4. *Cancer Research.* 2006; 66: 5624-5632.

- Hobbs, Christopher. *Foundations of Health: Healing with Herbs and Foods.* Interweave Press Inc., Loveland, CO. 1992.

- Hoffmann, David. *Medical Herbalism.* Healing Arts Press, Rochester, VT. 2003.

- Hoffmann, David. *Welsh Herbal Medicine.* Abercastle Publications: Ceredigion, UK, 1996.

- Jones, Eli. *Cancer, Its Causes, Symptoms & Treatment.* Boston, MA. 1911.

- Juge N, Mithen R, Traka M. Molecular basis for chemoprevention by sulforaphane: a comprehensive review. *Cell Mol Life Sci.* 2007 May; 64(9):1105-27.

- Kolpin D, Furlong E, Meyer M, Thurman E, Zaugg S, et al. Pharmaceuticals, Hormones, and Other Organic Wastewater Contaminants in US Streams. Environ Sci Technol. 2002; 36: 1202-1211.

- Kuch H, Ballschmiter K. Determination of endorcrine-disrupting phenolic compounds and estrogens in surface and drinking water by HRGC-(NCI)-NS in the picogram per liter range. *Environ Sci Technol.* 2001; 36: 3201-3206.

- Groff, J., Groper, S. & Hunt, S. *Advanced Nutrition & Human Metabolism (2nd Edition).* West Publishing Company, St. Paul, MN. 1995.

- Life Extension Foundation. *Disease Prevention & Treatment (4th Edition).* Life Extension Media, Hollywood, FL. 2003.

- Marieb, Elaine. *Human Anatomy & Physiology (4th Edition).* Addison Wesley Longman, Inc., New York, NY. 1998.

- Mills, Simon & Bone, Kerry. *Principles & Practice of Phytotherapy.* Churchhill Livingstone, New York, NY. 2000.

- Pitchform, Paul. *Healing with Whole Foods: Oriental Traditions and Modern Nutrition.* North Atlantic Books, Berkeley, CA.

1993.

- Pizzorno, Joseph. *Total Wellness*. Prima Publishing: Rockland, CA, 1996.

- Quitmeyer, Aimee & Roberts, Rebecca. "Babies, Bottles, and Bisphenol A: The Story of a Scientific Mother". *PloS Biol.* July; 5(7), 2007.

- Rauber, Paul. "Prozac River". *Sierra Magazine*. September/October 2007.

- Rose P, Huang Q, Ong C, Whiteman M. Broccoli and watercress suppress matrix metalloproteinase-9 activity and invasiveness of human MDA-MB-231 breast cancer cells. *Toxicol Appl Pharmacol.* 2005 Dec 1;209(2):105-113.

- Schnell, Nicholas. *Spring Liver Cleanse*. Self Published. 2000.

- Schnell, Nicholas. *Winter Kidney Cleanse*. Self Published. 2000.

- Schnell, Nicholas. *Fall Deep Tissue Cleanse*. Self Published. 2000.

- Sierra. January/Febuary 2008, page 19.

- Singleton D, Feng Y, Chen Y, Busch S, Lee A, et al. Bisphenol A and estradiol exert novel gene regulation in human MCF-7 derived breast cancer cells. *Mol Cell Endocrinol.* 2004; 221: 47-55.

- Skenderi, Gazmend. *Herbal Vade Mecum*. Herbacy Press, Rutherford, NJ. 2003.

- Tierra, Michael. *Planetary Herbology*. Lotus Press, Twin Lakes, WI. 1988.

- Vom Saal F, Welshons W. Large effects from small exposures II. The importance of positive controls in low-dose research on Bisphenol A. *Environmental Research.* 2006; 100: 50-76.

- Weiss, Rudolf. *Weiss's Herbal Medicine (Classic Edition)*. Thieme, New York, NY. 1985.

- Winston, David. *Herbal Therapeutics: Specific Indications For Herbs & Herbal Formulas (Eighth Edition)*. Herbal

Therapeutics Research Library, Inc. 2003.

- Winston, David & Kuhn, Merrily. *Herbal Therapy & Supplements: A Scientific & Traditional Approach.* Lippincott, New York, NY. 2000.

- Toyama Y, Suzuki-Toyota F, Maekawa M, Ito C, Toshimori K. Adverse effects of Bisphenol A to spermiogenesis in mice and rats. *Arch Histol Cytol. 2004; 67: 373-381.*

ACKNOWLEDGEMENTS

First, I want to thank the Great Mystery for the gift of creation and being able to serve my fellow man.

Thanks to mom and dad for being the best possible parents. Even though you haven't understood my fascination with natural medicine, you never judged me and have always supported me. To Pete (Medicine Eagle) Peterson. Thanks for teaching me about the Red Road. I wouldn't be here without you. To my beautiful wife Angie. You are everything I dreamed of and more. To my brother. I still look up to you. To my sister. For keeping me in line. To my grandparents, the biggest inspirations in my life. I still feel your guidance. Grandma, thanks for teaching me about the plants. Grandpa, thanks for the family lineage of the bear. To Aunt Millie. I hope I am as healthy as you the rest of my life.

To Miles my herbal brother. Thanks for being you and always being there. To Michael and Lesley Tierra. Thanks for teaching me, sharing with me, guiding me and providing me so many opportunities. To Master Chen. Thanks for allowing me to awaken my authentic spirit and sharing so many ancient mysteries. To Brian. Thanks for the clear vision of editing to this book. To all herbalists through time. Thank you for sharing your wisdom with me and inspiring me. To the plants themselves. Thank you for your egoless service to all mankind. To all my patients and friends. Thanks for teaching me about life and happiness.

CPSIA information can be obtained
at www.ICGtesting.com
Printed in the USA
FSHW011009070919
61778FS

9 781434 389862